Train Up A
In The Way He Should Go...

MW01097335

90 Day Bible Study / Prayer Guide for Children & Parents

GLORIA
HUNTINGTON

RuStir Publishing©

As A Gift For Your Child, Grandchild, Or Friend,
Leave A Special Note Here :

_____

_____

_____

_____

PREFACE

This 90 day nightly bible study and prayer book is written expressly to inspire new, or new-in-the-faith Christian parents. Psalm 119 is in the middle of the bible, it is the longest chapter in the bible. It is full of wisdom teaching us to love God's law, to write it on our hearts and to write it on the palms of our hands.

Repetition is key to learning God's laws so when your children are grown, they will not forget it because they have repeated it so many times. This is crucial for your children so when they are away from you and are afraid, worried, or concerned, they have the comfort of the Word of God to rely on.

Each day of teaching begins with a scripture directly from King James Bible Online .org text, then it has a summary from me. Next, there are prayers for you to share with your children so both of you are praying. There is a line for using your child/children's names in the prayer. At the end of the prayer we pray daily for God's Holy Land of Israel, our leaders, military and first responders to protect them, as God asks us to do.

After the prayer there is a question and discussion topic for you to encourage better understanding of the scripture and the prayer. Inside the middle watermark are sweet ideas to say goodnight, and share how special they are to you and to God.

It is with the utmost hope and love, I write these prayers for you and your children. Repetition is necessary to forge the bridge of safety of God's Word.

Be consistent and they will look forward to prayer time each night. God bless You!

Day 1 – Remember His Word

Scripture

My son, forget not my law; but let thine heart keep my commandments: For length of days, and long life, and peace, shall they add to thee. Let not mercy and truth forsake thee: bind them about thy neck; write them upon the table of thine heart: So shalt thou find favor and good understanding in the sight of God and man.

Proverbs 3:1-4 KJV

Gloria's Summary of Scripture

Learn the Word of God and keep it in your heart. Learn, listen, obey, and you will be blessed forever and ever.

KISS EACH FINGER ON EACH HAND
AS YOU BLESS
THE WORK OF THEIR HANDS

Prayer

Father God, bless _____ with health, happiness, and joy for You. Let them be warriors for You in all they do. Give them the zest for life You have, and for the life You've called them to do. Let them know You in all Your ways. Give them joy unspeakable and keep them safe in all they do. Keep them in Your hands, safely and full of health. God, love Your child as You show them Your mercies are new every morning. We include in prayer our President, our military men and women both home and away, all police officers and first responders in our daily prayers to keep them all safe and free from dangerous situations. We pray for Your Holy Land of Israel for peace in Jerusalem Lord. In Jesus' mighty name we pray, amen.

Questions & Discussion

Do you know why God wants you to keep His Word in your heart? Discuss keeping it close to you keeps you on the right path and from getting into trouble in all kinds of ways.

DAY 2 – LISTEN TO GOD

Scripture

My son, attend unto my wisdom, and bow thine ear to my understanding; That thou mayest regard discretion, and that thy lips may keep knowledge.
Proverbs 5:1-2 KJV

Gloria's Summary of Scripture

Learn what you can so you keep yourself in His will, listen and yearn to understand so you will know how to live.

HUG THEM TIGHTLY
SPEAK SOFTLY INTO THEIR EARS
I'LL LOVE YOU FOREVER

Prayer

Dear Jesus, we love You and ask You to give _____ the night's sleep they need. Give them sweet dreams and protect them from any nightmares that might come. Let them rest completely and wake up refreshed in the morning ready for a brand new day. Give them the joy of Your Spirit throughout the day and night. Let them be obedient each and every day, to want more understanding of how to walk with God daily. We thank You for hearing our prayers. We pray for peace in Jerusalem, wisdom and blessings for our President, our military home and away overseas, and all police officers, and emergency responders to be kept safe in all they do. We ask in Jesus' name, amen.

Questions & Discussion

Discuss last nights prayer and todays actions. See if there are any other questions.

DAY 3 – GOD'S WORD KEPT

Scripture

My son, attend to my words; incline thine ear unto my sayings. Let them not depart from thine eyes; keep them in the midst of thine heart. For they are life unto those that find them, and health to all their flesh.
Proverbs 4:20-22 KJV

Gloria's Summary of Scripture

God is always telling you to keep His word in your heart, to listen, and learn so you keep your eyes and heart pure. Doing this will give you better health in life.

> KISS THEM ON TOP OF THE HEAD
> TELL THEM
> YOU BLESS THEM IN THE
> NAME OF THE LORD

Prayer

Dear Jesus, We come to You in the name above every name. Jesus, on behalf of _____ We ask for Your guidance and leading so they will know You are always in authority over them. Lead them in a way they know You are helping and overseeing them as they go about their day. (Keep them safe under Your protection and give me guidance to always show them how much I love them and help me see their every need.) Thank You for Your promises and let them live with health as they follow your Word. May our President, our military, all police officers and emergency responders be safe in all they do. We pray for peace in Jerusalem, and we ask these things in Jesus' mighty name, amen.

Questions & Discussion

Why does a pure heart help us with our health? Discuss clean living as God intends keeps our health and minds strong.

DAY 4 – TRUST GOD

Scripture

Trust in the Lord with all thine heart; and lean not unto thine own understanding. In all thy ways acknowledge him, and he shall direct thy paths.
Proverbs 3:5-6 KJV

Gloria's Summary of Scripture

Lean on God for your every need and He will guide you to understand Him better and what He wants for you. Give Him the honor and glory for it and He will guide you through life.

TELL THEM TO CLOSE THEIR EYES
KISS EACH EYELID
TELL THEM TO SEE
THE GLORY OF THE LORD

Prayer

Dear Holy Spirit, _____ needs You to show them the way to behave and how to behave as they should in all aspects of their lives. (I ask for them to want to behave and to want to please You first, then me, as a parent. I ask for pleasant attitudes, willingness to obey quickly and for them to see the value of their work.) Lord, let them learn obedience is better than sacrifice. Let them keep these verses in their hearts as they better understand You. We are to pray for forgiveness for our sins and to repent of those sins. We pray for the safety of our President, our military, police and ask for them to be blessed. We pray for peace in Jerusalem, and we ask these things in Jesus' name, amen.

Questions & Discussion

Reassure them of your love, remind them the Father's love for them is even more than yours. Discuss this.

DAY 5 – GET WISDOM

Scripture

Get wisdom, get understanding: forget it not; neither decline from the words of my mouth.
Proverbs 4:5 KJV

Gloria's Summary of Scripture

To learn the Word of God is to gain wisdom and understanding. It will help us not to forget how we are to live.

KISS THEIR CHEEKS
LET THEM KNOW TO TURN
THE OTHER CHEEK IS GODLY

Prayer

Dearest Lord Jesus, tonight, we come to You, the author and finisher of our faith, asking for _____, and others in our home, and on our street, to learn of You in their homes and in the church. We ask each child be given an understanding of Your love and mercy, forgiveness, and tenderness for them. Let them see there is no love like Yours! (Let me shine as a light for You in their eyes.) Let them know love, mercy, and teaching as they grow in You and in the teaching here at home. We ask for our President, for our military men and women, the police, and first responders to be protected by angels in all they do. We continue to pray for peace in Jerusalem as you have asked Lord. In Jesus' name, amen.

Questions & Discussion

What does it mean to shine as a light? Discuss behaviors and what others see.

DAY 6 – UNDERSTAND CORRECTION

Scripture

My son, despise not the chastening of the Lord; neither be weary of his correction: For whom the Lord loveth he correcteth; even as a father the son in whom he delighteth.
Proverbs 3:11-12 KJV

Gloria's Summary of Scripture

Understand God will discipline you just as your parents do. Love is discipline; not punishment for doing wrong or making mistakes.

> HOLD THEIR HANDS
> TELL THEM THEY WILL ALWAYS
> BE ABLE TO TRUST YOU

Prayer

Dear Father God, Our Lord is the delight of our souls. We thank You so much for who You are, and for the blessings You have given us because we're Your children. As children of God, we have the same blessings You gave Jesus because we are joint heirs with Him, now grafted in as His adopted sons and daughters simply because You loved us that much. We ask _____ learns honor and obedience. We ask to learn quickly so discipline is not painful, but helpful to become the people You desired them to be from the beginning of time. Thank You Lord for Your faithfulness even when we are forgetful of all You've done for us. Lord, we want to be obedient in praying for Jerusalem, we ask for our President, military, police, and officers be kept safe. In Jesus' holy name, amen.

Questions & Discussion

God is love; He disciplines us when we don't follow his commands, just like how parents discipline when we do wrong. Talk about how we follow His way with teaching children.

Day 7 – Following Principles

Scripture

Hear, O my son, and receive my sayings; and the years of thy life shall be many. I have taught thee in the way of wisdom; I have led thee in right paths. When thou goest, thy steps shall not be straitened; and when thou runnest, thou shalt not stumble.
Proverbs 4:10-12 KJV

Gloria's Summary of Scripture

If you live as Jesus the Word tells you to live, you will be blessed and will not stumble as others would. Your path will be straight, and you will be protected.

Tell them to love others
as Christ loves them
follow with a big squeeze hug

Prayer

Dear Jesus, _____ and I come together in the name of Jesus for the opportunity to thank You for Your goodness as You willingly sacrificed Yourself on the cross for the forgiveness of our sins. Thank You Jesus! We ask You to teach them the basics of Who You are as they grow and learn more about You. Let them love You and have a healthy respect for what You've done and for Who You are God, our Friend and Creator. We ask for them to want to know You more and more, and hunger and thirst for Your righteousness. We repent of our sins. We ask for safety for our military home and away, for our President, all first responders and our police officers. We pray for peace in Jerusalem in Jesus' name, amen.

Questions & Discussion

Talk about how Jesus says your path will be straight and what it means for daily living and what the results of it are.

Day 8 – Hear Him

Scripture

Hear me now therefore, O ye children, and depart not from the words of my mouth.
Proverbs 5:7 KJV

Gloria's Summary of Scripture

Children let the Word of God fill you, so you never forget what He says.

KISS THE PALMS OF THEIR HANDS
THESE HANDS WILL DO
THE WORK OF THE LORD

Prayer

Dear Holy Spirit, remind us daily how much You love us. Remind _____ You're here with us to teach us every moment of every day. If we rely on You for our necessities in life, You won't ever disappoint us. Thank You for being here! We ask tonight, for Your tenderness to cover us, show us, shine through us, and teach us what You would have us know to follow You better. We want to be obedient children. Give them the knowledge they need to follow You and make good decisions. Give them Your grace as the day goes by. Tonight, let them sleep deeply with sweet dreams and allow them the visions You promised in Your Word. We pray for peace in Jerusalem, we ask for You to protect our President, our military, and our police from danger. Thank You, in Jesus' name, amen.

Questions & Discussion

What does it mean to be obedient? Explain "free will," and how it plays into decision making.

Day 9 – Live Right

Scripture

Keep thy heart with all diligence; for out of it are the issues of life. Put away from thee a froward mouth, and perverse lips put far from thee. Let thine eyes look right on, and let thine eyelids look straight before thee. Ponder the path of thy feet, and let all thy ways be established. Turn not to the right hand nor to the left: remove thy foot from evil.
Proverbs 4:23-27 KJV

Gloria's Summary of Scripture

Talk with clean lips, keep your eyes toward God, remind yourself where you're walking and keep yourself pure from sin.

HOLD THEM TIGHTLY
LET THEM KNOW THEY ARE FEARFULLY AND
WONDERFULLY MADE IN GOD'S IMAGE

Prayer

Dear Jesus, Your tender mercies are new every morning. You promised us to forgive all our sins. We always want to remember. Your faithfulness reaches to the heavens. We love You, Lord. We ask for _____ to lean on Your truths, learn Your ways, and remember Your values. We ask for them to want to please You in everything they say or do. Let us always remember Your loving kindness is so great no matter what we do, You will forgive if we just ask. Help us ask. We pray together for the safety and protection of our President, our military home and away, and police officers and emergency responders. We continue to pray for peace in Jerusalem, all In Jesus' name we pray, amen.

Questions & Discussion

What does it mean to always be truthful? Explain they can always come to you for forgiveness no matter what they have done, just as the Father forgives us. Discuss how discipline is done accordingly in love.

DAY 10 – GET UNDERSTANDING

Scripture

A wise man will hear, and will increase learning; and a man of understanding shall attain unto wise counsels: To understand a proverb, and the interpretation; the words of the wise, and their dark sayings.

Proverbs 1:5-6 KJV

Gloria's Summary of Scripture

In order to get understanding from a Proverb, or the Word of God, you will have to read it, hear it, apply it, and live it. It comes with a promise from God to help you all the way.

LET THEM KNOW
THEY MAY DISAPPOINT YOU SOMETIMES
BUT THEY CAN ALWAYS TRUST YOU
AND TELL YOU ANYTHING

Prayer

Dear God in heaven, Father, You are not only our heavenly Daddy, but You're also a Father so loving and kind, we sometimes forget just how wonderful You are. Help _____ not to forget! Let _____ remember You're the Creator of all the universe and You are our Friend who sticks closer than a brother. We can talk to You about anything. Let them see Your hand in their lives as You give them guidance through all the growing periods of life. Let them be a shining light for Your kingdom! Oh Lord, let them be used for Your magnification and glory in all they say and do, forever. We pray for our President, military, and police for their protection and for angels to keep them safe. We pray for peace in Jerusalem. Thank You, in Jesus' name we pray, amen.

Questions & Discussion

What does this mean for your future? God honors His promises and hears your prayers.

DAY 11 – LEARN QUICKLY

Scripture

Turn you at my reproof: behold, I will pour out my spirit unto you, I will make known my words unto you.
Proverbs 1:23 KJV

Gloria's Summary of Scripture

God will pour out His spirit on you once you learn His Word. He will supply all your needs because He is great and can be trusted.

GIVE THEM A KISS
ON TOP OF THE HEAD
GENTLY STROKE THEIR HAIR AND LET
THEM KNOW HOW MUCH YOU LOVE THEM

Prayer

Dear Jesus, my Redeemer, You have loved us from the beginning of creation, in Genesis when man and woman were created. Lord, please help _____ remember how much You love us. You love us so much; You were obedient to go to the cross in order to die and rise again so we could be saved. You saved us! We want to be thankful for what You did. Help us each day to remember our blessings. Help us learn the bible and remember what You said. We repent daily of our sins, Lord. Thank You for Your faithfulness to forgive. We continue to pray for peace in Jerusalem Lord, we pray for the President, military who keep us safe to be blessed, and our police's protection as they work to keep our neighborhoods safe. In Jesus' name we pray, amen.

Questions & Discussion

Explain how sometimes we expect our prayers to work quickly and they are on God's timing, so He answers when the timing is right.

DAY 12 – TRAINING

Scripture
Train up a child in the way he should go: and when he is old, he will not depart from it.
Proverbs 22:6 KJV

Gloria's Summary of Scripture
Just as the military trains their soldiers every day, we too shall be trained and you will forever know His protection from the enemy that is out to steal, kill, and destroy.

GIVE THEM A KISS ON THEIR FEET TOPS
TELL THEM THEY WILL WALK WHERE
THE LORD WANTS THEM TO GO

Prayer
Dear Jesus, our Redeemer, in all we do, we thank You. You are our salvation, our healer, our Friend, and our helper in all times of trouble. We ask for _____ to learn Your training quickly. We pray they are warriors for You in all they do. We pray they have hearts for You and love You with all their hearts. Let them know how much You love them daily. We thank You Lord for Your faithfulness. We pray for the President because You said to pray for our leaders. We pray for our military men and women who keep us safe, and for our police officers, and first responders to be protected too. Continued prayer for peace in Jerusalem. Praying in the name above every name, Jesus, amen.

Questions & Discussion
This scripture is the title of the book, it is that important. Discuss why it is so important to your child, and give them opportunity to respond with their thoughts.

Day 13 – Sing His Praises

Scripture

Praise ye the Lord. Sing unto the Lord a new song, and his praise in the congregation of saints. Let Israel rejoice in him that made him: let the children of Zion be joyful in their King. Let them praise his name in the dance: let them sing praises unto him with the timbrel and harp. For the Lord taketh pleasure in his people: he will beautify the meek with salvation. Let the saints be joyful in glory: let them sing aloud upon their beds.

Psalms 149:1-5 KJV

Gloria's Summary of Scripture

God delights in singing and dancing children. He glories in their delights and pleasures. Sing, dance, and love the Lord. You can even sing in your bed!

KISS THEM ON THE TIPS OF THEIR NOSES
TELL THEM GOD MADE THEM
JUST LIKE THEY ARE AND
HE LOVES THEM

Prayer

Dear Heavenly Father, we do delight in You. We thank You for all our blessings; some of which we take for granted. We choose to always be thankful for what You have provided. You want _____ to learn to be thankful and appreciate the many blessings they have. We want to teach them those things we do naturally come from You. Thank You Lord! We pray for the military away from home who are defending our way of life, our President who needs wisdom, and our police officers and first responders who have dangerous jobs. We pray for our leaders as You instructed us. We pray for peace in your Holy Land of Israel Lord. We pray in Jesus' holy name, amen.

Questions & Discussion

Do you sing out loud? Dance around the house? Let them see you be silly and enjoy a song together.

DAY 14 – LEARN & REMEMBER

Scripture

The fear of the Lord is the beginning of knowledge: but fools despise wisdom and instruction. My son, hear the instruction of thy father, and forsake not the law of thy mother.
Proverbs 1:7-8 KJV

Gloria's Summary of Scripture

Fearing the Lord doesn't mean to be afraid. It means to be fully aware that He is the mighty God Who should be highly important in your life. Only foolish people refuse to listen to God.

KISS EACH EAR
WHISPER FOR THEM TO LISTEN
TO THE SMALL STILL VOICE
OF THE LORD

Prayer

Dearest Lord Jesus, teach _____ the lesson of knowing a healthy fear of God; not the fear that God will hurt them, but know God is holy and therefore, He is worthy of being praised and adored. Help us all learn it. We ask for them to be mighty, shining examples of Christians, are helpful to others, forgiving and full of repentance when they do something wrong or make mistakes. God loves a willing child and we ask they be ever ready to give themselves and help others at any time. We want to learn to repent quickly, apply ourselves to learning Your Word, and to live according to Your will. Teach us, Lord. We pray as You have requested for our President, our military, and our police to be safe and protected. Praying for peace in Jerusalem. We pray in Jesus' name, amen.

Questions & Discussion

Explain how God is not to be feared because He would not hurt us, He is the final authority on everything we do. Discuss how God spoke His Word in the bible too!

DAY 15 – SEVEN THINGS GOD HATES

Scripture

These six things doth the Lord hate: yea, seven are an abomination unto him: A proud look, a lying tongue, and hands that shed innocent blood, An heart that deviseth wicked imaginations, feet that be swift in running to mischief, A false witness that speaketh lies, and he that soweth discord among brethren.
Proverbs 6:16-19 KJV

Gloria's Summary of Scripture

God is the source of everything good and He has seven things described in the scripture He hates. A proud attitude, a lying tongue, murder of the innocent, a wicked imagination, one with bad behavior, false storytelling, and starting conflicts between people.

> KISS THEIR WRITING HAND
> (IF YOU KNOW IT)
> THIS HAND WILL DO MIGHTY WORKS
> FOR GOD

Prayer

Dear Lord God, help _____ know the things that make God angry. There are many things that make Him happy, but sometimes we do things without thought and we want to repent for them: for instance not to be prideful or proud, such as a smirk face, being truthful, because no lie is ever good. Causing the shedding of innocent blood is wicked, such as murder. A wicked imagination can be planning revenge; keep us from this evil. Help us be careful to mind our own business, and Lord, help them always accurately report anything they see and to keep from gossip with others. These things are not of God and we thank You Father You're always willing to forgive our sins. We pray for our President, our military, first responders, and the police's safety, peace for Jerusalem all in Jesus' name, amen.

Questions & Discussion

Ask them how many of the seven things off the tops of their heads can they remember after the prayer.

Day 16 – Clean Mouth & Mind

Scripture

Hear; for I will speak of excellent things; and the opening of my lips shall be right things. For my mouth shall speak truth; and wickedness is an abomination to my lips. All the words of my mouth are in righteousness; there is nothing froward or perverse in them. They are all plain to him that understandeth, and right to them that find knowledge.
Proverbs 8:6-9 KJV

Gloria's Summary of Scripture

Keep your mouth clean in all you say. To God, swearing is ugly. Keep your words on good things and teach others you will never speak in a way that makes God unhappy.

> KISS THEIR THROATS
> THE WORDS THAT COME FROM YOUR
> THROAT TO YOUR LIPS
> WILL SPEAK LIFE

Prayer

Dear Holy Spirit, teach us Your ways in all we do. Help us please God in all the words we use. Let _____ remember our clean lips and pure heart make God happy because we honor Him that way too. Help us speak clearly, without dirty words, or dirty thoughts. Help us honor God! Let us learn filthy words hurt God's feelings especially since so many times those words use His name in vain. Give us hearts to speak pleasantly in all our ways. Remind them to be careful when they are tempted to say words that will hurt others, especially words that hurt God. We pray for forgiveness and repent. Thank You Lord Jesus and fill us again with Your Holy Spirit. We pray for our President, our military and our police to be safe and protected, and for peace in Jerusalem. In Jesus' precious name, amen.

Questions & Discussion

"When I was a child, I spoke as a child…" Yes, even some adults use dirty words and have impure thoughts, explain how we try hard not to use them or be around those who do.

Day 17 – Receive Wisdom

Scripture

Receive my instruction, and not silver; and knowledge rather than choice gold. For wisdom is better than rubies; and all the things that may be desired are not to be compared to it. I wisdom dwell with prudence, and find out knowledge of witty inventions. The fear of the Lord is to hate evil: pride, and arrogancy, and the evil way, and the froward mouth, do I hate. Counsel is mine, and sound wisdom: I am understanding; I have strength.

Proverbs 8:10-14 KJV

Gloria's Summary of Scripture

Money, or jewels are unimportant in God's world. He would much rather you learn wisdom and control your tongue. He is the all-important teacher of all good things. He will give you wisdom if you ask.

> LISTEN TO THEIR CHESTS
> DRUM OUT THE RHYTHM
> TELL THEM THE HEARTBEAT
> IS FROM GOD HIMSELF

Prayer

Dear Jesus, give us wisdom! Give _____ understanding of the importance of living a clean life and going through life learning the heart of God. These things learned early will enhance our lives in every way. Thank You we can read the Word, understand what is written and learn each day. Thank You we're teachable. Let us remember money and jewels are unimportant to God. Yes, He provides our needs and He always will, and when we repent of any sin, He forgives for those sins. Thank You Jesus we can come to You and You are faithful and just to forgive and love us. We want to be obedient in praying daily for peace in Jerusalem, our President who needs wisdom, our military for safety, our police officers, and all first responders protection. We pray in Jesus' name, amen.

Questions & Discussion

Talk about the importance of money, but how it is not to become an idol, how we give the gifts of jewels (like a diamond ring) and why these are precious to us but how wisdom is more important.

Day 18 – Seek God Early

Scripture

I love them that love me; and those that seek me early shall find me.
Proverbs 8:17 KJV

Gloria's Summary of Scripture

Get up in the morning and pray. If you love Him, you will find it becomes easier to do with practice.

TICKLE THEIR KNEES
LET THEM KNOW
GOD LOVES A
KNEELING PRAYER WARRIOR

Prayer

Dear God, Oh Lord, You are such a faithful God! Every morning Your mercies are new. Help _____ to seek You early in the morning when we get up and our day will go so much better! Early in life, it is easier to learn these principles to make a rich life, valuable in blessings and giving glory to God. Give us the wisdom to seek You daily. Every day we ask we get up with a good attitude, one of gratitude because You are the supplier of everything we need during the day. Help us be thankful for our blessings. Help them be helpful to their teachers, parents and neighbors. Reward them with Your many blessings. We pray for our President, our military who protect us, and our police who need Your help every day. We pray for peace in Jerusalem in Jesus' name, amen.

Questions & Discussion

Make a plan. Have them hold you accountable to take a minute before breakfast, during the two minutes of brushing teeth, maybe on the car ride to school...acknowledge God and praise Him to start the day.

DAY 19 – GOD WATCHES

Scripture

A soft answer turneth away wrath: but grievous words stir up anger. The tongue of the wise useth knowledge aright: but the mouth of fools poureth out foolishness. The eyes of the Lord are in every place, beholding the evil and the good.
Proverbs 15:1-3 KJV

Gloria's Summary of Scripture

Speaking softly to someone who makes you mad is a good idea. It's hard to do. If you become wise, you'll know this. Fools speak mindless things. God is watching all the time, knowing if you do evil or good.

TUSSLE THEIR HAIR
TELL THEM GOD EVEN
HAS THEM NUMBERED
THAT IS HOW MUCH HE LOVES US

Prayer

Dear God, help _____ know how much You love us and want us to succeed. When someone makes us mad, let us instantly know not to answer in anger, but reply softly. Yes, it's hard to do and it takes practice, but we know it can be done. Help us not to act or speak foolishly. Help them know the truth, because the truth is Your Word. It's biblical! God is always watching. Show us how not to be fearful but rejoice knowing we are pleasing You in all we say and do. Give us wisdom in all we do. Growing in the knowledge of the Lord is good for us for all sorts of reasons. Help us keep that in mind as we live day by day. Lord, we pray for peace in Jerusalem, we pray for our President, our military, and police to be safe and protected. In Jesus' name, amen.

Questions & Discussion

How should you reply when you are mocked or insulted? Explain what today's culture teaches and why those are not God's principles. Let the light shine.

Day 20 – Laughter Is Good

Scripture

A merry heart doeth good like a medicine: but a broken spirit drieth the bones.
Proverbs 17:22 KJV

Gloria's Summary of Scripture

A merry heart, or a happy spirit, is good medicine. The fact is laughter is good for you. It releases chemicals in your brain that stimulate your body to return to health. A person who doesn't laugh or enjoy comedy has dry bones that are brittle and can easily break.

> Kiss each tops of the shoulders
> God gave these to you to lift
> Heavy things you will work for
> Him as He calls you

Prayer

Dear Jesus Christ, our Savior, let _____ always be happy and merry in attitude. Let us know the joy of our salvation. Remind us laughter at the right and proper things is such good medicine! Help us be merry and enjoy the blessings of life. Joy is different from happiness because joy comes from knowing the Lord. Help us be joyful and full of merriment. Smiles are contagious! A merry heart is what we want. Let us know Your joy and share it with others throughout our lives. We pray for our President, for our military, and our police as they're all safe and protected, and for peace in Jerusalem. We ask for forgiveness of our sins and repent. Thank You Lord for Your faithfulness. We pray in Jesus' name, amen.

Questions & Discussion

Have you ever told a dirty joke? Better to laugh from the depth of the belly with clean humor. Explain how good stories, clean jokes and fun with others is important but must stay clean to honor God.

DAY 21 – COMMIT TO GOD

Scripture

The preparations of the heart in man, and the answer of the tongue, is from the Lord. All the ways of a man are clean in his own eyes; but the Lord weigheth the spirits. Commit thy works unto the Lord, and thy thoughts shall be established.

Proverbs 16:1-3 KJV

Gloria's Summary of Scripture

In everything you do, commit to God to do your very best. He knows your heart. He knows if you want to please Him, or if you want to please people. Our intentions are one thing, but God knows them either way.

KISS THEIR CLOSED EYELIDS
SEE WHAT GOD
SHOWS YOU TOMORROW

Prayer

Dear God, You are faithful and just. You are kind and generous to Your children, believers in Jesus Christ our Lord and Savior. We ask You prepare _____ heart to be kind, as You are kind. Let our voices be soft and pleasing to You. We want to commit our very souls to You, our words, our bodies be the living sacrifices You've asked us to do in following Your example. Jesus was the ultimate sacrifice, and we too can learn to sacrifice for Your glory. We don't want to sin; we want be worthy of Your love and devotion. Thank You for teaching us these values. Help us know and commit to God fully every day. We pray for the President, our military and the police, and emergency responders to be safe and protected. We pray for the peace of Jerusalem. Praying in Jesus' holy name, amen.

Questions & Discussion

Why is Jesus worthy of our praise and thanks? Discuss these things to express how out of these come great blessings. Without thanks and giving you will not experience true joy.

Day 22 – Be Humble

Scripture

By humility and the fear of the Lord are riches, and honour, and life.
Proverbs 22:4 KJV

Gloria's Summary of Scripture

Riches are fleeting unless they're from God. His values are not the values most people enjoy but the promises that follow them are eternal. God will give you a long, healthy life if you are humble and not proud.

AS YOU TUCK THEM IN TELL THEM
I LOVE YOU TO THE MOON AND BACK
IF THEY RESPOND I LOVE YOU MORE
PLAY THAT GAME

Prayer

Dear Jesus, my Helper and Friend, let _____ rejoice in the goodness of our Lord Jesus. He is kind, compassionate, loving and forgiving. We praise Him because He first loved us. Before we knew Him, He loved us. Thank You for calling us into Your kingdom. We ask for humility—not being boastful about anything. We know we've done nothing of ourselves, but everything good comes from You. Help us be thankful, humble and glorify You in all we do. Help us be kind, like You are. Help us be truthful, like You are. Help us be loving everywhere we go. We lift You up Lord, because You are worthy. We ask for forgiveness of our sins as we repent and pray. Bless our President, our military and police to be safe and avoid danger. We pray for peace in Jerusalem in Jesus' name, amen.

Questions & Discussion

If we turn our thoughts to our emotions we can become depressed that we don't "measure" up. We are to look to Jesus for "happiness" and be humble/meek/gentle. Talk about how to do that and what it looks like in daily life.

Day 23 — Evil Is Not Rewarded

Scripture

Fret not thyself because of evil men, neither be thou envious at the wicked; for there shall be no reward to the evil man; the candle of the wicked shall be put out.

Proverbs 24:19-20 KJV

Gloria's Summary of Scripture

God keeps score, for lack of a better word. He knows when we've sinned, or when He's pleased. We should never envy what wicked people have or want to be like them in any way. God promises believers in Jesus will have rewards, but evil people will face a fiery pit in hell.

TUCK THEM IN TURN OFF THE LIGHT
SPEAK SOFTLY I LOVE YOU MORE TODAY
THAN YESTERDAY
BUT NOT AS MUCH AS TOMORROW

Prayer

Dear Jesus, glory and honor and blessings to Your name. There is no greater name than Jesus. Thank You for Your death on the cross for us and our redemption. Lord, help _____ want to be like You in every way, not supporting evil or evil people. Help us understand the principle of rewards in heaven for our obedience. Those evil people will have no rewards. They will have nothing to look forward to, but Christians will! We have the promises of God and He is faithful to perform every one of them. Thank You God for helping us grow in Your ways and learn faithfulness. Give us Godly vision, words, thoughts and deeds. We ask for forgiveness of our sins and we repent for them. Lord, we pray for your Holy Land of Israel, for peace in Jerusalem. We pray for our President, the military, and the police for their safety and to keep them out of dangerous situations. We pray in the name of Jesus, amen.

Questions & Discussion

Is God a spy? Of course not, He carefully watches over us to keep us safe, protects us and reminds us to stay on His path. He would never hurt us, He is LOVE!

DAY 24 – BE LIKE GOD

Scripture

My son, give me thine heart, and let thine eyes observe my ways.
Proverbs 23:26 KJV

Gloria's Summary of Scripture

If you want to be like God, then learn and live His ways. That's why you always learn His Word and keep it in your heart. Observe His ways and you will prosper.

WHISPER WORDS OF AFFIRMATION
I THINK YOU ARE SPECIAL
YOU ARE LOVING
AND YOU ARE KIND

Prayer

Dear God, keep _____ in Your will as we move about and keep Your Commandments. Always keep us in Your will. We want to please You and serve You to the best of our abilities. Let us learn to grow in Jesus, grow in good deeds, grow in serving others, grow in faithfulness, grow in goodness. Your way is the only way, O God. Give us the knowledge to be wise! Years don't matter; what matters is the condition of the heart. Let our hearts be tender for You in all ways. Keep us safe through life, encourage us and show us Your goodness because of our faithfulness to Your principles and laws. We pray for forgiveness for sins and repent of them. We pray for our President, our military men and women, police officers, first responders, and for the peace of Jerusalem. In Jesus' name, amen.

Questions & Discussion

Ask if they want to commit their whole hearts to God right now. If they haven't yet, ask. Write down the date and time in the front of the book.

Day 25 – Talk Less Listen More

Scripture

A fool uttereth all his mind: but a wise man keepeth it in till afterward.
Proverbs 29:11 KJV

Gloria's Summary of Scripture

Foolish people talk too much, sometimes all the time. Wise men keep quiet. If there is something important to say, there is a time to speak up. Otherwise it is best to gain wisdom and just listen.

KISS THEM ON THE FOREHEAD
SPEAK WORDS OF TRUTH
YOU ARE SOMEONE
VERY IMPORTANT TO GOD

Prayer

Dear God, Lord, keep _____ lips pure and holy. It can be hard to do, but we can do it with Your help. We can learn how to use self-control and self-discipline. It won't hurt us to sacrifice a little control for the sake of our souls. It blesses us if we control our tongues. Lord, give us the ability to control our tongues, even in school. Give us the ability to exercise control every day until we establish ourselves as true and faithful followers of our Lord and Savior, Jesus Christ. Help us speak peaceably and gently to our friends. Even when kidding, our mouths can get us in trouble. Help us know the difference. We give You all the credit for being able to control our tongue. We give You all the glory. We ask for safety for our President, military, police, and we pray for the peace of Jerusalem. Thank You, Lord, in Jesus' name, amen.

Questions & Discussion

Discuss talking too much versus asking questions to learn because there is a difference. Not to talk...just to talk, it is good manners and polite to let others talk. They will learn when it is important to speak up.

DAY 26 – GOD'S WORD IS PURE

Scripture

Every word of God is pure: he is a shield unto them that put their trust in him. Add thou not unto his words, lest he reprove thee, and thou be found a liar.
Proverbs 30:5-6 KJV

Gloria's Summary of Scripture

God doesn't need a reminder His Word is pure truth. But He promises to shield and protect those Christians who believe and trust His Word. He warns adding anything to the bible or putting your thoughts and words above His will cause you to be a liar.

BUTTERFLY KISSES ON THE CHEEK
THIS LITTLE FACE
IS WONDERFULLY MADE

Prayer

Father God, remind _____ You made promises You faithfully keep. Your Word is pure, it is truth and it is life to our bones. Give us understanding. When people put themselves, their ideas, or their agendas before Yours, they are found to be liars. You said so. Let us realize this fact and move beyond it to the point of excelling in it. Let us know, comprehend and understand the facts presented here. Grow us in the saving knowledge of Your grace and mercy. Let us recognize error when we see it. There are many cults today who think they know better than God but those are lies. Let us fully know Your Word to offer words of truth to those who might change the bible or alter it in any way. It is perfect as it is! We pray for our President, our military, and safety for our police, and we pray for the peace of Jerusalem as You taught us to pray, in Jesus' name, amen.

Questions & Discussion

In our culture there are changes in attitudes toward holiness. Ask them for an example where they have seen this. Discuss it and remind them to praise God in all things and be light to others.

Day 27 – Work Hard

Scripture

He that tilleth his land shall have plenty of bread: but he that followeth after vain persons shall have poverty enough.
Proverbs 28:19 KJV

Gloria's Summary of Scripture

Life is about Him. It isn't about us. That means we are called to work so we have food to eat. Biblically speaking, people who don't work don't eat. God blesses those who work hard.

MAKE A COMMENT YOU KNOW
THEY WILL APPRECIATE
YOU WERE SO SWEET
WHEN YOU DID _____ TODAY

Prayer

Dear Jesus, help _____ know good work ethics. Help them grow in the spirit of working for You, not working for a boss. Our efforts are solely to please You and when we do, we learn righteousness follows if we work hard and dedicate our work to You. All things good will follow. Let them learn this principle early. They can take out the trash, make the bed, do the dishes, help with dinner, simple tasks and more as they grow. Let us learn this worthwhile effort. Help us learn You are the ultimate boss, One Who loves us more than any earthly boss ever will. We ask our attitudes be adjusted to recognize this. We repent for attitudes less than full of gratitude. Blessings and honor to You O God. We pray for our President, military, and the police to be safe. We continue to pray for the peace of Jerusalem. Praying in our Lord Jesus' name, amen.

Questions & Discussion

Who likes hard work? It is good for us; explain how it teaches us lessons and it is also good to rest, but not be lazy. Adults work for a living, and children work to learn things as they grow.

DAY 28 – FIRST COMMANDMENT

Scripture

And God spake all these words saying, I am the Lord thy God, which have brought thee out of the land of Egypt, out of the house of bondage.

Exodus 20:1-2 KJV

Gloria's Summary of Scripture

God reminded the people of His greatness by saying "I Am" He that brought them out of a terrible situation. I Am is used every time you tell someone what you are called. You use His name! He is talking about His Ten Commandments in this verse.

LET THEM KNOW
HOW MUCH YOU APPRECIATE THEM
DOING PRAYERS AT NIGHT

Prayer

Dear God, O God of our fathers, the One Who is called Great and Mighty, we thank You for being the One True God. We love You because You first loved us. It is a wonderful thing You have done for us. As believers, we thank You daily for the blessing of salvation. Let _____ learn of Your greatness and Your holiness. Give us knowledge beyond our years. We will love You and serve You all our days. Give us the tools we need to follow You. Let us shine for You. Give us love for one another as You have called us all to do. We ask for forgiveness of our sins and we turn away from them in repentance. We pray for the peace of Jerusalem, for our President, the military, and the police, and emergency responders to be protected as they serve the people. In Jesus' holy name, amen.

Questions & Discussion

Pick one of the Ten Commandments and discuss what it means and why it is so important. If you need help, Google it together for an image and let them pick one to talk about.

DAY 29 — NONE OTHER

Scripture
Thou shalt have no other gods before me.
Exodus 20:3 KJV

Gloria's Summary of Scripture
God is a jealous God, and He's allowed to be because He is The Holy One. He desires our love more than we'll ever know. He wants us to put Him first in all we do, and nothing else will ever compare to Him, in any way.

KISS THE TOP OF THEIR HEAD
REMIND THEM THIS BRAIN IS
GOD'S TO USE
AS HE WILL IN JESUS' NAME

Prayer
Dear God, You alone are God. _____ repents of sins Lord. We have made idols out of things You don't approve of. We have accidentally done it too. Sometimes we just don't think spiritually. Forgive us Father God. You are worthy of all praise, glory, honor, thanks, blessings and power. Let the children know Who You are in majesty and magnificence. Our God, the Holy One of Israel is the True God Who is worthy of our praise. God, help us understand the importance of obeying Your Word. Teach us to change into the people You desire. Help all of us from the inside out. You alone are the One God. We give You thanks. We pray for our President, our military, the police officers for their safety, and for the peace of Jerusalem. We pray in Jesus' name, amen.

Questions & Discussion
Why is God jealous? Explain how He guides us so we don't lose our paths and life is better for us. He wants all of our attention so when we stray, He misses out on spending time with us just like we can be jealous if a friend spends more time with others.

DAY 30 – NO IDOLS

Scripture

Thou shalt not make unto thee any graven image, or any likeness of any thing that is in heaven above, or that is in the earth beneath, or that is in the water under the earth: Thou shalt not bow down thyself to them, nor serve them: for I the Lord thy God am a jealous God, visiting the iniquity of the fathers upon the children unto the third and fourth generation of them that hate me; And shewing mercy unto thousands of them that love me, and keep my Commandments.
Exodus 20:4-6 KJV

Gloria's Summary of Scripture

God is a jealous God. Only He is worthy. Idols made and worshiped is an abomination to Him, a direct insult to His holiness. The penalty for this is sin passed down to the children in the third and fourth generations.

LEAN THE CHILD FORWARD
SCRATCH THEIR BACK SAYING
I PRAY FOR YOUR GROWTH
AND HEALTH IN JESUS' NAME

Prayer

Dear Father God, let us begin our prayer by thanking You for the opportunity to confess our sin. We have cherished things that meant nothing really, yet You were offended. Teach _____ to repent. It is a good thing to be disciplined so we don't do it again. Forgive us. Lord, reach down into our souls and teach us the good from the bad as we read Your Word. Teach us to love Your laws, Your Word, Your promises and help them learn how much You love them, being human, we often forget. As the Almighty Savior, change our hearts to please You. We pray for the peace of Jerusalem. We pray for our President, our military, and the police for continued safety in dangerous situations. We pray in Jesus our Lord's name, amen.

Questions & Discussion

What in the home could be an idol? Is it a figurine, a doll, maybe the TV show, or even the money in your piggy bank? How does your heart feel toward these things, if you live for or want them more than Jesus, you worship an idol. Repent of this and be free.

DAY 31 – DO NOT SWEAR

Scripture

Thou shalt not take the name of the Lord thy God in vain; for the Lord will not hold him guiltless that taketh his name in vain.
Exodus 20:7 KJV

Gloria's Summary of Scripture

Using God's name in vain means using it to swear, cuss, or use vulgarity in connection to His mighty name. It's meant to be an insult to God. God promises wrath in connection to using His name that way.

TUCK THEM IN TIGHTLY
SEE IF THEY CAN WIGGLE OUT
MAKE IT FUN
KISS THEM GOODNIGHT

Prayer

Dear God, _____ and I sincerely apologize for using Your name any way other than to exalt You. We repent. It was never our intention to insult You, but out of ignorance, we have. Thank You for Your forgiveness! It means everything to us. Lord, we ask for clean mouths, clean hearts and clean hands. Let everything we say and do reflect Jesus in our lives. Let us shine for You, O Lord. You are great, and greatly to be praised. We truly are grateful You forgive our sins. We're free from concern over our sins because they've been erased, thanks to Your mercy. We pray for our President to have wisdom, our military to be safe, our police officers to be protected, and we pray for the peace of Jerusalem. In Jesus' name, amen.

Questions & Discussion

We have discussed this topic earlier, but it is a Commandment so God must not like it. Talk about how using His name in any other way that is negative or not appropriate for little ears. Know it displeases God and hurts His heart.

DAY 32 – DAY OF REST

Scripture

Remember the sabbath day, to keep it holy.
Exodus 20:8 KJV

Gloria's Summary of Scripture

The sabbath day, or Saturday, has changed to Sunday church. He said to rest on the sabbath, now Sunday, keeping yourself in holiness. He meant it for our refreshment, so we have a full week to spend our day praising and appreciating Him.

KISS THEM
HUG THEM
LET THEM KNOW YOU LOVE TO SEE
THEM ALWAYS TRY

Prayer

Dear God, O Lord, there have been days we worked hard on the sabbath. We've had days we get caught up in our lives and don't take the time to glorify You. We repent of this and ask for Your forgiveness. We understand You are the One we're supposed to appreciate on holy days, plus daily living. Life isn't about us; it's about You. Help us remember our time on earth is to honor and share the gospel. Change our minds and hearts, O Lord. You are worthy of our thanks and praise. We ask _____ learns this faster than the adults have and remember to keep it holy. We pray for our President, our military, the police for divine protection, and we pray for the peace of Jerusalem. In Jesus' name, amen.

Questions & Discussion

What does it means to rest? Sleep, or watch TV, or playing with friends? Sunday after attending church, take the day to praise and glorify Him, using the day to pray and build family relationships.

DAY 33 – HARD WORK THEN REST

Scripture

Six days shalt thou labour, and do all thy work.
Exodus 20:9 KJV

Gloria's Summary of Scripture

Another of the Ten Commandments: it is repeated tonight If we have a day of rest, Sunday, our sabbath, then we should honor it after the other six days of hard work to keep food on the table and a bed to rest our heads.

GIVE THEM KISSES ON THE EYES
THESE EYES ARE
THE WINDOWS OF YOUR SOUL
BLESS THEM LORD

Prayer

Dear God, Lord after a long week of hard work, help us remember to rest rather than play selfishly. Help us wind down so we're prepared for a day of refreshing. Let _____ know in our hearts how important this is, and for honoring God. We want to be obedient to Him and this is how we rest up and learn more about Him and His goodness. We repent of taking the day away from Him. We pray for a hungry heart. We pray for our souls to hunger and thirst for the things God has. The closer we draw to Him, the closer He comes. Thank You Lord for another opportunity to learn. We pray for our President, our military, the police and ask for their protection. We pray for the peace of Jerusalem. In Jesus' holy name, amen.

Questions & Discussion

Creating habits: talk about what your plans are for this coming Sunday and how you will choose to honor the Sabbath and work hard the rest of the week.

DAY 34 – REMEMBER GOD

Scripture

But the seventh day is the sabbath of the Lord thy God: in it thou shalt not do any work, thou, nor thy son, nor thy daughter, thy manservant, nor thy maidservant, nor thy cattle, nor thy stranger that is within thy gates: For in six days the Lord made heaven and earth, the sea, and all that in them is, and rested the seventh day: wherefore the Lord blessed the sabbath day, and hallowed it.
Exodus 20:10-11 KJV

Gloria's Summary of Scripture

On the seventh day when God rested, He had made everything, looked at it and called it good. He made a day of rest for Himself and if we are created in His image, and we are, then surely we can take one day to remember Him.

ANOINT THEIR HEADBOARD
MAKE A SMALL CROSS WITH OLIVE OIL
FOR A PEACEFUL SLEEP
LET THEM KNOW JESUS HONORS THE OIL

Prayer

Dear Lord our God, we love a day set aside for rest. _____ and I will use the day to love You, to love each other and to follow Your plan for our lives. We make things hard and so we apologize and ask for forgiveness for taking a day away from You. We know whatever You have set, it must be for our good. Everything You do is for our good. You are a good God Who knows what we need even before we do. You alone have the wisdom to lead people where they need to go. We ask we're open to Your will for our lives, no matter the direction. Help us be willing to be willing. We pray for the peace of Jerusalem, the safety of our President, our military, and the police. In Jesus' name we pray, amen.

Questions & Discussion

Again REST! He really desires you rely on Him for everything and when we give up our will to God He shows us just how much it works. He even teaches in repetition for our learning. God is so good.

DAY 35 – HONOR

Scripture

Honour thy father and thy mother: that thy days may be long upon the land which the Lord thy God giveth thee.
Exodus 20:12 KJV

Gloria's Summary of Scripture

God's promise here is to honor your parents, no matter how hard it may be, and if you do, you will live a long life. It comes with a promise.

POINT TO THEIR BELLY BUTTON
EXPLAIN HOW THIS IS WERE THEY
ATTACHED IN THE WOMB FOR FOOD

Prayer

Dear Father God, help _____ be faithful in honoring their mother and father daily. We forget sometimes and we are not honorable, please help us be better. We want to remember You made a promise if we do honor our parents, we will live a long time. We must decide daily to honor them and we will. Thank You for this. We want to honor You too. Forgive our sins and wash us clean. Thank You, Lord. We continue to pray for the peace of Jerusalem, we also pray for protection for our President, our military's men and women both home and away, and the police officers and all first responders. In Jesus' name, amen.

Questions & Discussion

What does the word honor really mean? It is not to hurt others but to lift them up, be obedient, timely, courteous, and be a servant for God. Treating others as we would like to be treated is honoring them with the "golden rule." He promises a long life for it.

DAY 36 – DO NOT KILL

Scripture

Thou shalt not kill.
Exodus 20:13 KJV

Gloria's Summary of Scripture

This Commandment is using the word "murder" for kill. It is always wrong to purposely murder someone. What is allowed though, is to defend yourself. That's different.

TURN OFF THE LIGHT
ASK IF THEY HAVE ANY FEAR
LET THEM KNOW THE ROOM HAS ANGELS
PROTECTING THEM AS THEY SLEEP

Prayer

Dear God, You have said murder is wrong, _____ and we understand. What isn't mentioned here though, is to even consider for a moment that thought in our minds is wrong too. If we think about murdering someone, it's the same to You as if we did it. We repent for our thoughts too. You're such a big God You even forgive people who do this wrong act. We thank You for Your forgiving tender loving kindness and mercy. Thank You for the reminder our thoughts must be pure too. We pray for the peace of Jerusalem, the protection for our President, our military, and police. We pray in Jesus' name, amen.

Questions & Discussion

This Commandment from God was a direct order: do not murder. He knows in times of war it is different. Explain how not all people are Christian; but our country must protect us from evil and protect other places too.

DAY 37 – STAYING FAITHFUL

Scripture

Thou shalt not commit adultery.
Exodus 20:14 KJV

Gloria's Summary of Scripture

Some children grow up with cheating parents. This Commandment is explaining that God is displeased with that behavior, regardless of the "explanation" behind it. Parents are to love one another and respect the commitment they made to each other.

ASK FOR A GOOD STORY
FROM THEIR DAY
LISTEN CAREFULLY
THANK THEM FOR SHARING

Prayer

Dear God, we choose every day to be faithful to our spouse, to our children and to You. We make this choice upon our own convictions that this is the right way to behave. We make the proper choices every moment of every day to act and behave in a righteous manner in all situations. Help _____ understand our daily choices determine our happiness factors later. There are consequences for sin because our sins will find us as they always do. Thank You Lord, You are merciful and full of grace. You gave us this Commandment so we stay fulfilled and happy because we choose to do the right thing. We continue to pray for the peace of Jerusalem, the divine safe protection of our President, our military, police, and first responders. We pray in Jesus' name, amen.

Questions & Discussion

Choices are around us daily. Tell them if we dwell on something long enough there is a good chance we will do whatever it is we think about. Discuss how it can hurt others.

DAY 38 – IT'S NOT YOURS

Scripture

Thou shalt not steal.
Exodus 20:15 KJV

Gloria's Summary of Scripture

Sometimes some adults steal. Children may start with something small they want to have; it's part of the human condition. Once it is successful, it can happen often. Put a stop to it now as being a thief is a sin.

WIGGLE THEIR TOES
THESE LITTLE PIGGIES ARE PERFECT
BECAUSE GOD MADE THEM
(PIGGY GOES TO THE MARKET STORY)

Prayer

Dear Lord God, we have all stolen something that wasn't ours to take. Whether in secrecy, in the darkness, or without being aware, it remains a sin. You've called us to stop that behavior and we must. If it isn't ours, we can offer to buy it, and that may work, but if not, then it remains in the possession of another. Remind _____ we have no right to take things from someone. We have no right to keep something we've found without trying to find the owner. Let us always remember stealing is theft and You don't like thieves. We put away this sin and thank You for taking away the desire. Precious Lord, You are our healer. Heal us from this wayward behavior. We pray for the protection of your Holy Land of Israel, for peace of Jerusalem, protection and wisdom for the President, our military, and the police to be safe too. In our Lord Jesus' name, amen.

Questions & Discussion

Teach them if they ever steal something you will make them return it with apologies. It is a powerful message to lead by example, no matter the reason. If it isn't theirs they need to know without permission it is theft.

DAY 39 – LYING IS A SIN

Scripture

Thou shalt not bear false witness against thy neighbour.
Exodus 20:16 KJV

Gloria's Summary of Scripture

If you witness an accident or wrongdoing, explain it to the proper authority correctly without adding or omitting anything. Be truthful in telling the whole truth.

KISS THEIR CHEEKS
WHEN YOU'VE DONE EVERYTHING
YOU KNOW TO DO
PRAY AND JUST TRUST IN JESUS

Prayer

Dear God, embellishments often happen. We stretch the truth to become a lie. We've all done it. We've told "fish" stories that aren't completely true, or "little white lies." Forgive us for those. _____ thanks You when we ask for forgiveness, You are faithful and just to forgive our sins as You've promised. We will not change facts, but only report them as we witnessed them. We want to remember these truths every chance we get to tell a witnessing story. Remind us if we're ever given the opportunity to report something. We pray for the peace of Jerusalem as You've requested, the safety of our President, our military, and the police officers and emergency responders who protect us. We pray in Jesus' mighty name, amen.

Questions & Discussion

What is a liar? Even "little white lies" are lying and God forbids lies. This Commandment reminds us NO lying, gossip or telling an untruthful story about others is good. It hurts people. Adults don't respect others who lie. Telling the whole truth is Godly.

Day 40 – Not Yours To Desire

Scripture

Thou shalt not covet thy neighbour's house, thou shalt not covet thy neighbour's wife, nor his manservant, nor his maidservant, nor his ox, nor his ass, nor any thing that is thy neighbour's.
Exodus 20:17 KJV

Gloria's Summary of Scripture

If it's not yours, don't covet—want it. You can want something "like" it, but not what belongs to the neighbor's "others."

Ask if the child has anything
to be concerned about
Discuss it with love
and understanding

Prayer

Dear Lord God, our eyes are the windows of the soul and since they see things they like, please remind us some things are off limits for us. We can buy something much like what they have, but we don't ever want what belongs to others. Help us recognize the difference. If we think on these things, it can become a desire, so help us to move past the lust of the eyes. Give _____ the recognition their friend's toys are not for them. They might borrow them, or trade for them or just enjoy playing together. Help them see we must ask for forgiveness for anything we have done that is not pleasing to You Lord God. Thank You for forgiving us. Tonight, we want to pray for the peace of Jerusalem, the protection of our President, military, and the police who continue to protect us. In Jesus' name, amen.

Questions & Discussion

Explain this Commandment is important to God. He gives us what we need, not what others need or have. Explain the difference between borrowing and stealing.

DAY 41 – WAITING

Scripture

But they that wait upon the Lord shall renew their strength; they shall mount up with wings as eagles; they shall run, and not be weary; and they shall walk, and not faint.
Isaiah 40:31 KJV

Gloria's Summary of Scripture

Waiting for anything is an unknown and can be very hard. God asks us to wait on Him. We will be stronger for learning lessons by waiting on God and the right things will bless you because of it.

> HELP THEM HEAR JESUS
> SHHH CLOSE YOUR EYES AND
> JUST LISTEN FOR A MINUTE
> JUST 60 SECONDS IN SILENCE

Prayer

Dear Jesus our God, we understand waiting is hard. We have waited, even if it was "just a minute." We're not used to waiting and liking it. Help us Lord, change _____ attitudes towards waiting on You. Waiting to grow up is hard enough, so help us get through all things and continue to show us Your promises. We want our strength renewed daily while we are learning to wait. We want to soar like eagles, to always be protected but with freedom while we wait. We want to run and not be tired, walk and not faint, as scripture says. Help us grow in patience while we're waiting. We pray for the President to have wisdom, our military home and away to have protection of angels, the police officer and first responders to be protected in dangerous situations. We pray for peace in Jerusalem in Jesus' name, amen.

Questions & Discussion

Talk about walking in love and patience while waiting on God. Be anxious for nothing but grateful for everything. God's timing is perfect and we can't see what His plan is. We will be blessed when we wait on Him.

Day 42 – Life Here And After

Scripture

For God so loved the world, that he gave his only begotten Son, that whosoever believeth in him should not perish, but have everlasting life.
John 3:16 KJV

Gloria's Summary of Scripture

Belief in Jesus' death on the cross means you are a Christian with the promises from God to follow you. He will give you power through His name, and authority over spiritual things, as well as life in heaven forever.

Cup their ears with your hands
Let them know to
Listen closely so they hear what
God has to tell them tonight

Prayer

Dear Jesus, _____ has made You Lord and Savior because we believe in Your death on the cross, Your resurrection after three days, and Your rising to heaven with the promise You will return for us. We are excited to see what You have built for us in heaven when the time comes. Because we know You, and we're learning Your principles, help us retain what we learn and learn more every day. It is a challenge everyday living in the world, thank You for helping us remember You are forgiving, loving, kind, truthful, faithful and always merciful. Forgive our sin and help us establish Your principles in our lives. We pray for the peace of Jerusalem, the protection of our President, our military, and our police. In Jesus' name we pray, amen.

Questions & Discussion

Why did Jesus die on the cross? Who did He do it for? Does He need to do it again? Discuss what happens to us when we die.

DAY 43 – GO, TEACH, BAPTIZE

Scripture

Jesus said, "Go ye therefore, and teach all nations, baptizing them in the name of the Father, and of the Son and of the Holy Ghost: Teaching them to observe all things whatsoever I have commanded you: and, lo, I am with you always, even unto the end of the world. Amen.
Matthew 28:19-20 KJV

Gloria's Summary of Scripture

Jesus gave us a command to spread the gospel by using verbs to make His point: go, teach, baptize, teach to observe. You'll see He places emphasis on teaching. Each of us is commanded to share the gospel.

KISS THE LITTLE ONE ON THE LIPS
WITH A BIG SMACKING SOUND
AND SAY
I LOVE THOSE KISSES

Prayer

Dear Holy Spirit, Lord, we have neglected Your commandment to go and spread the gospel and we are so sorry. We repent and ask for Your forgiveness. Please help _____ share the good news anytime we can! This news is eternally good, and we are sorry we have forgotten to share it with strangers, family, friends, and whoever we meet. Help us understand the importance of it. You are our helper in times of trouble, and sometimes we get shy or feel others might not understand what we're trying to say. Help us understand it's not up to us to get them ready, but it's up to You to prepare their hearts. You get them where they need to be. We just plant a seed. Thank You God You have saved us. We love You. We also pray for the protection of the President, our military, the police, and pray for the peace of Jerusalem. In Jesus' name, amen.

Questions & Discussion

Do you know anyone who needs Jesus? We all do, talk about how you can easily talk to them about God and see if they want to go to church with you. It all starts by planting a seed.

DAY 44 – LOVE IS EVERYTHING

Scripture

Master, which is the great commandment in the law? Jesus said unto him, Thou shalt love the Lord thy God with all thy heart, and with all thy soul, and with all thy mind. This is the first and great Commandment. And the second is like unto it, thou shalt love thy neighbour as thyself.
Matthew 22:36-39 KJV

Gloria's Summary of Scripture

The simplicity of love is something so extraordinary we often miss it. Jesus fulfilled the Ten Commandments into just two; love God and love others.

> IN A SOFT VOICE LET THEM KNOW
> HOW MUCH YOU LOVE WITH A HUG
> SPENDING TIME WITH THEM
> AND GOD TOGETHER

Prayer

Dear Jesus, our Master, help _____ love one another as You've commanded us. That means everyone including people who are not easy to love. It means the grumpy ones, people of all colors, mean bullies, and those like the homeless who aren't clean. You love them. It's up to us to treat them like You do. Help us love God with our whole hearts, minds, souls, and teach others Who He is. If we learn love, we will have had a good life! Help us know love, but also be aware of bad things around us. We must learn caution too. We know God is with us wherever we go, but we must pay attention to our surroundings. We must learn to share the gospel to others with love. Help us do that too. We pray for the peace of Jerusalem, the protection of our President, our military, and the police to be free from danger. We pray in our precious Jesus' name, amen.

Questions & Discussion

How can you show love to other people? Make a plan to spend a day serving others somehow. However you choose, help them bless other people. It will give them great joy and gratitude.

Day 45 – The "Be" Attitudes

Scripture

Blessed are the poor in spirit: for theirs is the kingdom of heaven. Blessed are they that mourn: for they shall be comforted.
Matthew 5:3-4 KJV

Gloria's Summary of Scripture

God has blessed those who have lowered their self-importance in spirit. He gives them the kingdom! He is God, all glory and honor is His. Those who are hurting and not feeling like they are worth anything will be comforted by God and that is His promise.

TOUCH THEM WITH YOUR
FINGERS ON THEIR TEMPLES
KISS THEM ON THE FOREHEAD AND
WHISPER I THINK YOU'RE SO SMART

Prayer

Dear Jesus, You've promised to give the kingdom of heaven to people who are humble in spirit. Help _____ please You that way. Help us comfort people who are sad because someone died, or because their lives are messy. Help us be Your hands to do Your work, have a heart like Yours and be Your helpers during these hard times with other people. You are always here to help, so we count on that for ourselves, but help us be there for other people when they need it. Give us a good attitude. Give us the attitude to be helpful to others even when we don't know we're helping. Bless us with love for one another Lord. We pray for the protection of our President, our military, police officers, and first responders, and we pray for the peace of Jerusalem. In Jesus' name, amen.

Questions & Discussion

A "be" attitude is a great way to show how we should behave. These next few nights we will explore the different ways to act. God blesses the well behaved.

Day 46 – The "Be" Attitudes

Scripture

Blessed are the meek: for they shall inherit the earth. Blessed are they which do hunger and thirst after righteousness: for they shall be filled.
Matthew 5:5-6 KJV

Gloria's Summary of Scripture

Meek people are not weak. They are strong, but quiet and lowly in spirit. God says they will have the earth, meaning they will be with God when He takes back the world! He blesses those who really want to be morally good and promises emotional fullness.

> Give them something to remember
> get on your knees
> By the Spirit of the Lord
> bless this child amen

Prayer

Dear Jesus, _____ wants to be like You too. We want to be humble and meek so You're pleased with us. You promise good things to people who are obedient to Your Word and values. Help us grow in obedience to these principles. We want to inherit the earth. We want Your blessings because we hunger and thirst for righteousness. We know if we seek You out, You will be found, and You will give us the desires of our hearts. Righteousness is to be morally good and it isn't how most of the world is now, but we know You will bless us if we are meek, and You will make us full when we follow Your Word. Thank You Lord for teaching us these things. We pray for the peace of Jerusalem, for the protection and safety of our President, our military, and the police. In our Lord Jesus' name, amen.

Questions & Discussion

Did you know we are royalty? We are sons and daughters of the King! We are to have attitudes of righteousness and we will be blessed beyond measure.

DAY 47 — THE "BE" ATTITUDES

Scripture

Blessed are the merciful: for they shall obtain mercy. Blessed are the pure in heart: for they shall see God.

Matthew 5:7-8 KJV

Gloria's Summary of Scripture

God asks us to be forgiving. That way, when we need forgiveness, we will receive it too. He asks us to be pure in heart, so we see God. Not everyone will see God right now, but it's a great reminder of how to "be."

SHOW THEM JUST HOW MUCH
GOD LOVES THEM
(STRETCH OUT YOUR ARMS WIDE)
THAT HE STRETCHED OUT HIS ARMS
AND DIED FOR THEM

Prayer

Dear Jesus and Holy Spirit, there are days when _____ is not forgiving, gracious, compassionate, or merciful to others, please forgive us. There are days when we're not pure in heart, forgive us. We ask forgiveness of sins we've committed because we didn't know. We are accountable for the things we know, and we thank You for teaching them to us. Help us live and do and be as You have commanded us. Help us give mercy to people who have hurt us, meaning to or not. Help us be pure in heart so we don't sin. We know we will sin, but we should not mean to. We understand You will forgive us quickly if we ask. We need mercy for wrongs we didn't mean to do, and Your mercy is there. Thank You for providing it for us because You love us. We are praying for the peace of Jerusalem, safety of our President, our military, and police. In Jesus' name, amen.

Questions & Discussion

Do you know what mercy is? God excels in mercy. He gives us grace for making mistakes and children need to know this, but doesn't mean to take advantage by doing things just to ask forgiveness. Explain and discuss this.

Day 48 – The "Be" Attitudes

Scripture

Blessed are the peacemakers: for they shall be called the children of God. Blessed are they which are persecuted for righteousness' sake: for theirs is the kingdom of heaven.
Matthew 5:9-10 KJV

Gloria's Summary of Scripture

Everyone is called to be a peacemaker. Situations come up that need someone who knows how to make peace. Being persecuted and harassed is becoming more common in our country. We understand this. In the Last Days Jesus is preparing a place for us in heaven.

GIVE YOUR BLESSINGS TO THEM
JESUS LOVES YOU
I LOVE YOU THE MOST I CAN BUT
HE LOVES YOU MORE

Prayer

Dear God, being a peacemaker is a gift and we acknowledge it. _____ wants the gift. We want to know we are children of God. We want to be blessed as we're persecuted for being a Christian and give us the courage to stand up for You. We understand those days are happening and we want to be better prepared for it. Help us put on the armour of God from Ephesians 6 to stand in the days of persecution. We will inherit the kingdom of heaven when we stand for righteousness. Help us do it even when we feel we can't. Thank You Jesus for giving us this special gift. We pray for the President, our military, the police officers, and all emergency responders to be protected from danger, and we pray for the peace of Jerusalem. In Jesus' name, amen.

Questions & Discussion

What does it mean to armour up? Apply it daily --- the armour of God is spiritually protecting yourself from the world's evil. Peace makers are special to God and He calls them children of God. Mockers will make fun of you for loving Jesus, but we get forever gifts for it in Heaven.

DAY 49 – THE "BE" ATTITUDES

Scripture

Blessed are ye, when men shall revile you, and persecute you, and shall say all manner of evil against you falsely, for my sake. Rejoice, and be exceeding glad: for great is your reward in heaven: for so persecuted they the prophets which were before you.
Matthew 5:11-12 KJV

Gloria's Summary of Scripture

God says you're blessed when men mock you and say ugly things about you, persecute you for your faith, and blame you falsely for things you didn't do or say. He says to rejoice and be glad. You will have a reward in heaven.

HUG THEM AND SAY
I AM SO PLEASED YOU'RE MINE
NO ONE ELSE CAN EVER FILL YOUR
SPOT IN MY HEART

Prayer

Dear Jesus, You were persecuted. Your prophets were persecuted. How can _____ expect to go through life without being persecuted just because we love and follow You? We can't. It is expected. Please help us be strong and get through these hard times. With Your help, we can do anything. We can overcome this when we daily put on the armour of God and pray, seek You and walk in accordance with Your Commandments. Lord, we count on You to get us through when asking for Your help, and You will come through because You are faithful all the time. The Holy Spirit will be there for every trial that comes our way. We pray for the peace of Jerusalem, wisdom for our President, our military, and the police to be safe from dangerous situations. We pray in Jesus' name, amen.

Questions & Discussion

Tonight repeats last night. Discuss how you can rejoice in the trials, how you can embrace the persecution knowing in the end...God WINS, WE WIN!

DAY 50 – ARMOUR UP

Scripture

Finally, my brethren, be strong in the Lord, and in the power of his might. Put on the whole armour of God, that ye may be able to stand against the wiles of the devil.
Ephesians 6:10-11 KJV

Gloria's Summary of Scripture

When you dress for battle, you need to armour up and put on your gear. We are in a battle we can't see; it is a spiritual battle. The amour of God will help us in the day to day battles we face.

> KISS THE CHILD AND SAY
> I COULD ONLY LOVE YOU MORE IF WE
> LIVED IN HEAVEN

Prayer

Dear God, Lord please help _____ learn what spiritual battles are all about. Teach us what we need to know so we don't go without our battle gear on. Help us understand the scriptures that teach us about spiritual war. Help us stand strong in the battle instead of sinning and making mistakes that don't honor You. We need to know we don't have to run or hide. We should stand, steadfast in You, and put the devil on the run instead. Thank You Lord, these principles are easy for children to understand too. We don't need to freeze in fear because we know the fear of the Lord will put thousands to flight. We know You are here with us. We pray for the peace of Jerusalem, the protection of the President, our military home and away, the police to be safe from danger. In Jesus' mighty name, amen.

Questions & Discussion

In the next few nights, we will continue to discuss the armour of God. Build excitement toward the different armour to apply daily. For tonight, just pray they are ready to remember the importance of it.

Day 51 – Stand In Armour

Scripture

For we wrestle not against flesh and blood, but against principalities, against powers, against the rulers of the darkness of this world, against spiritual wickedness in high places. Wherefore take unto you the whole armour of God, that ye may be able to withstand in the evil day, and having done all, to stand.
Ephesians 6:12-13 KJV

Gloria's Summary of Scripture

There are demons in the atmosphere just waiting to find a hole in your battle gear. Principalities are a type of demon, powers are strong demons, and rulers are just that. They're high up in the atmosphere and come to earth during sin, and are given the way in.

KISS THE TOP OF THEIR HEAD
I HAVE SO MUCH TO BE THANKFUL FOR
—— YOU ——

Prayer

Dear God, Thank You Lord for helping _____ understand this concept. We may not understand it fully now, but we want to. We don't want to be ignorant of what is going on around us. Sometimes we accidentally let spirits in when we're completely clueless about what is happening. We know the devil is always busy and we know he is always trying to ruin us. So, help us get this information in our spirits so it's easier for us to understand. The battle is real. Help us be ready every day and night. We want to always be prepared wearing armour for these battles! We pray for the peace of Jerusalem, the protection of the President, our military, and the police. In Jesus' name, amen.

Questions & Discussion

Where do you think you can "see" these demons? Maybe in TV, movies, games where there is evil and killing? We are to protect and guard our eyes and minds.

DAY 52 – FULL ARMOUR

Scripture

Stand therefore, having your loins girt about with truth, and having on the breastplate of righteousness; And your feet shod with the preparation of the gospel of peace; Above all, taking the shield of faith, wherewith ye shall be able to quench all the fiery darts of the wicked. And take the helmet of salvation, and the sword of the Spirit, which is the word of God.
Ephesians 6:14-17 KJV

Gloria's Summary of Scripture

When we put on the full armour, we've protected our minds, our chests, our loins, our feet and a shield is faith and our sword is the Word of God. Only the blood of Jesus can protect us more! We never remove our armour, we keep applying it daily.

> RUB THEIR LITTLE SHOULDERS
> WHISPER IN THEIR EARS FOR THEM TO
> LEARN TO REST MY CHILD
> JESUS WILL TAKE CARE OF YOU

Prayer

Dear God, as we dress for spiritual battle, we've taken steps to protect ourselves with Your armament and Your Word. We can also apply the blood of Jesus over us as we go onward. In serious times of trouble, You are there to see us through. We thank You for that promise, and You are faithful to all Your promises. _____ wants to learn how to battle, how to pray and how to live through these trials that come even when we're walking with You. Teach us how to do this daily and how to armour up for battle. Thank You Jesus for this as we pray for our President, our military, the police for their protection, and for the peace of Jerusalem. In Jesus' name we pray, amen.

Questions & Discussion

This is it! It is all the battle gear you need to live without fear of the enemy. Take up each piece daily for protection and pray without stopping. Repent often so your peace is not destroyed.

DAY 53 – DAILY PRAYER WARRIOR

Scripture

Praying always with all prayer and supplication in the Spirit, and watching thereunto with all perseverance and supplication for all saints; And for me, that utterance may be given unto me, that I may open my mouth boldly, to make known the mystery of the gospel, For which I am an ambassador in bonds: that therein I may speak boldly, as I ought to speak.
Ephesians 6:18-20 KJV

Gloria's Summary of Scripture

Asking God for the things you need should become second nature. He is here to supply them for you. He wants us to ask boldly, go forth boldly, to speak plainly and with authority to the people we meet.

DANCE AROUND THE ROOM
(AS IF THE CHILD IS IN YOUR ARMS)
I FEEL LIKE DANCING...
THIS IS HOW HAPPY YOU MAKE ME

Prayer

Dear God our Father, _____ wants to keep praying with boldness for the things we need and for You to supply according to Your riches in Christ Jesus. We ask for our mouths to obey our minds and do what You've called them to speak. We want obedience. We ask for Your truths to flow through our minds, hearts and souls and to fill us with all righteousness in Jesus. When we do, we'll be in Your will for our lives and You will be pleased with us. You said we don't have because we don't ask, so we are asking. As we learn to walk in this new instruction, help us understand what it means as we go about doing the Lord's work. We ask for protection for our President, our military, the police, all first responders, and for the peace of Jerusalem. In Jesus' name, amen.

Questions & Discussion

Tell them THANK YOU for being a daily prayer warrior, for being consistent talking with God and strengthening their relationship with Him. They will not part from it.

DAY 54 – LORD'S PRAYER

Scripture

After this manner therefore pray ye: Our Father which art in heaven, Hallowed be thy name.
Matthew 6:9 KJV

Gloria's Summary of Scripture

He is the Father of us all. He lives in heaven and He lives in us through His Holy Spirit, which is often confusing. He is three in One. God the Father, Jesus the Son and the Holy Spirit. God's name is holy no matter which of His many names You use.

GIVE KISSES AND HUGS
THANK YOU FOR BEING ALL MINE
I SHARE YOU WITH JESUS
BUT HE GAVE YOU TO ME

Prayer

Dear God, Your names are holy. We call You Father, the Holy One of Israel, many more we don't know yet. We want to please You. We desire You are enjoying our journeys as we go through life trying to get it right. We want to. Help _____ choose the narrow way every time. When we get off the right path, teach us and correct us how to get back where we need to be. You are in heaven with the many people who have gone to heaven. You are with the angels and the creatures in heaven. You're very busy but we know You always have time for us. Thank You for showing us how to pray and ask for the things we need and you always supply. We give you praise. We pray for the peace of Jerusalem and the protection of our President, our military, and the police. We pray in Jesus' name, amen.

Questions & Discussion

The beginning of the Lord's Prayer. Learn this verse tonight...repeat it again and again out loud. Tomorrow night add to it the next verse.

DAY 55 – LORD'S PRAYER

Scripture

Thy kingdom come. Thy will be done in earth, as it is in heaven.
Matthew 6:10 KJV

Gloria's Summary of Scripture

Jesus taught we should ask for His kingdom to come. We honor each time we ask Him to return to earth. Any time we ask His will to be done in earth, it is that way in heaven too.

WE WANT YOU TO REMEMBER THIS
NO ONE
NO ONE BUT JESUS COULD LOVE YOU
MORE THAN WE DO

Prayer

Dear God, help _____ learn the whole prayer and pray as Jesus taught us. It's Your will for our lives and we want to be obedient to prayer too. We want Jesus to come for us and take us to heaven. We want to be with Him forever in heaven. What we ask for in earth is in line with Your will, Your Word and the thing we ask for will be done in earth as it is in heaven. We look forward to perfection in heaven. We want our prayers to be in the perfect will of God. Help us learn, as we grow, we know You will make everything more clear. We ask for the peace of Jerusalem, the protection of our President, our military home and away, and all police officers. We pray in the name of Jesus, amen.

Questions & Discussion

Memory lessons of this simple prayer prove fruitful, so continue to put them together for the complete prayer. This is how the Lord teaches us to pray, so its important to learn.

Day 56 – Lord's Prayer

Scripture

Give us this day our daily bread. And forgive us our debts, as we forgive our debtors.
Matthew 6:11-12 KJV

Gloria's Summary of Scripture

Jesus taught we're supposed to ask God for our daily food. He's also referring to the bread as the Word of God. We have debts to other people, and they have debts to us. Let us forgive them as He forgives us, but means we still must repay a loan.

KISS YOUR CHILD'S ARMS
THESE ARMS WILL CARRY MANY THINGS
I BLESS THEM
FOR GOOD THINGS

Prayer

Dear Jesus, help us ask You for each meal we need, because You have supplied from Your riches in heaven. We mean to ask for Your bread, the bread of Life—Jesus too. We want to remember to do that every day. We know people borrow things, because we do too. But when we forget to return them, we owe the person an extra kindness when we do return them later. It pleases You to do this. We must always remember things we owe must be paid on time as it is expected. Help us do what is right in all things. We ask for the peace of Jerusalem, the safety of our President, our military, and the police in times of danger. We pray in Jesus' name, amen.

Questions & Discussion

We want to pray for food and before meals each day. Practice taking turns so they can see how it is done. Explain debts and how we pay our bills monthly.

Day 57 – Lord's Prayer

Scripture

And lead us not into temptation, but deliver us from evil: For thine is the kingdom, and the power, and the glory, for ever. Amen.

Matthew 6:13 KJV

Gloria's Summary of Scripture

Finally, Jesus said to avoid things that tempt us, because it will keep us from danger and evil. The kingdom is His and the power is His and the recognition or glory is His forever.

KISS YOUR CHILD'S CHEEK
WHATEVER GOD WANTS YOU TO BE
IS
WHAT I WANT YOU TO BE TOO

Prayer

Dear God, when we remember who has the power, the glory and the might to remove evil from us, we'll be in a great position to pray for others. We praise You too. _____ gives You all the praise because You made this world and everything in it. We thank You. We thank You for forgiving our sins and teaching us how to avoid doing the same mistakes again. Help us learn this prayer and apply it to our lives every day. We continue to pray for Your Holy Land of Israel Lord, for the peace of Jerusalem, for the protection of our President, our military home and away, and the police officers and emergency responders. We pray in the name of Jesus, amen.

Questions & Discussion

What is your biggest temptation? Ask God for help to keep us from sin, danger and evil from the devil.

Day 58 – Golden Rule

Scripture

"The golden rule"—Therefore all things whatsoever ye would that men should do to you, do ye even so to them; for this is the law and the prophets.
Matthew 7:12 KJV

Gloria's Summary of Scripture

This rule means whatever someone does to you in kindness, do to them. If someone is cruel to you, this means you don't return evil for evil. You give back kindness. We are to be like Jesus and love others the way He loves us.

GIVE A BIG WIGGLY HUG AND SING
JESUS LOVES YOU THIS I KNOW
FOR THE BIBLE TELLS ME SO
LITTLE ONES TO HIM BELONG
THEY ARE WEAK BUT HE IS STRONG

Prayer

Dear Jesus, Lord please help _____ understand better how to treat everyone like Jesus does. It's easy to be nice to someone when they've been nice to us, but it's hard to be nice when they haven't. Help us be nice all the time. Help us show the kind of love to others You would have shown if that happened to You. Remind us all the time, through Your Holy Spirit we should be thankful, loving, kind, helpful, sweet, truthful and appreciate someone else's efforts. We continue to pray for the peace of Jerusalem as You have asked Lord, for the protection of our President, our military, and the police. We pray in the name of Jesus, amen.

Questions & Discussion

Revisiting the "golden rule"—remind them how to treat others; we don't hold grudges and we forgive those who treat us unfairly. We treat them just like Jesus would because He is watching, He always knows, so let's please Him. Love others.

Day 59 – Idle Words

Scripture

But I say unto you, That every idle word that men shall speak, they shall give account thereof in the day of judgment.
Matthew 12:36 KJV

Gloria's Summary of Scripture

Ouch! This is serious. Everything we say may be meaningless or pointless, without feeling for others, or just babbling away is dangerous. We must consider everything we say should have a purpose for good.

GO OVER TODAY'S LESSON
ASK IF THERE ARE ANY QUESTIONS
EXPLAIN HOW PROUD YOU ARE THEY
ARE LISTENING TO THE WORD OF GOD

Prayer

Dear God, we say things just to talk sometimes. We didn't know it was wrong. We're sorry, we apologize for babbling foolish things. Help _____ to always do better. Help us not to speak worthless words or roll our eyes. Help us not complain about things we don't want to do. Help us be better when our parents tell us to do something we may not want to do, especially if they say to do it "now." Help us so we keep from getting into trouble. Help us learn this now so we don't have to stand in front of You and explain it. We pray for the peace of Jerusalem, for the protection of our President, our military home and away, and the police officers and first responders. We pray in the name of Jesus, amen.

Questions & Discussion

Explain how we are to be quiet listeners to gain knowledge and wisdom unless we have something important to say. We can't get ugly words back.

Day 60 – Becoming An Adult

Scripture

When I was a child, I spake as a child, I understood as a child, I thought as a child: but when I became a man, I put away childish things.

1 Corinthians 13:11 KJV

Gloria's Summary of Scripture

Putting away one's childhood can be hard. When your kids become teens, they like to think they're grown, but we know better. When they are adults, they will better understand what this scripture is all about.

KISS HUG AND WHISPER
IT IS GONNA BE A GREAT DAY
FOR YOU TOMORROW BECAUSE
YOU HAVE JESUS WITH YOU

Prayer

Dear God, we are kids! Lord please help _____ to have wisdom beyond our years for Your principles and how to use them. We know we don't think like adults, but we will someday. We don't want to make too many mistakes. We want to please You and grow in Your Word and Your ways by reminding, encouragement, prayer and help along the way. Let Your Holy Spirit do His work in us. Give us knowledge beyond our years. Help us figure out what needs to be done so we don't make as many mistakes. Help us throughout our journey, Lord Jesus. We pray for the peace of Jerusalem, for the protection and wisdom of our President, our military, and police. We pray in the name of Jesus, amen.

Questions & Discussion

Talk about growing up too fast, they have their whole lives to be adults and Jesus loves His children. They must learn lessons along the way, but it is important not to skip these years.

DAY 61 – GOD IS MIGHTY TO SAVE

Scripture

I will love thee, O Lord, my strength. The Lord is my rock, and my fortress, and my deliverer; my God, my strength, in whom I will trust; my buckler, and the horn of my salvation, and my high tower. I will call upon the Lord, who is worthy to be praised: so shall I be saved from mine enemies.
Psalms 18:1-3 KJV

Gloria's Summary of Scripture

God is our strength. He says He is our rock, he's a fortress—a place to go that is very strong, He is our deliverer, we can trust Him, One to grab onto in trouble, a high tower or a place others can't go and he who calls upon the Lord will receive help from enemies.

ASK YOUR CHILD TO BOW THEIR HEAD
AND SAY A SHORT PRAYER FOR YOU
(GET THEM USED TO IT)

Prayer

Dear God, _____ loves You, Lord. You are teaching us these principles with love and mercy. You are worthy of all the praise. Your name is higher than any other name. You alone are the Creator and You're our Friend. You give us everything and we are thankful. We want to remember to thank You for keeping us safe from our enemies, safe from harm and safe as we walk through life. Thank You for the promise You will watch over us and we can come to You any time; even always. You've called us to pray for our leaders and for the peace of Jerusalem. We want to honor those in leadership above us. We pray for the President for safe keeping and guidance to make wise decisions; have him lean on You for understanding, for our police, and our military to be kept safe and free from danger. We pray in Jesus' name, amen.

Questions & Discussion

This is a powerful prayer that should be prayed often, it speaks highly of Who He is and what to do when in trouble. Discuss what "the Lord is my rock" means.

Day 62 – No Other Name

Scripture

Neither is there salvation in any other: for there is none other name under heaven given among men, whereby we must be saved.

Acts 4:12 KJV

Gloria's Summary of Scripture

This scripture couldn't make it more plain if it was tattooed on our foreheads. There simply is no other name. Jesus is the only person by which to be saved. Remember He has many names, but it must be only by His name.

Tickle them on the tummy
I pray this tummy will have food
to nourish you and to keep
you well throughout your life

Prayer

Dear Heavenly Father, with all the names out there from other religions, salvation isn't through any name but Jesus. _____ is also saved because of what He did on the cross. He died for our salvation and our adoption into the kingdom of heaven. His blood was shed for us. He became sin so we could be forgiven and go to heaven if we believed on Him. Thank You for the provision You gave us to get into heaven. We believe! Lord, salvation is ours because we believe in Jesus. We believe He is the Son of God; He is our Redeemer and our Righteousness. Thank You God for giving us Your Son. Help us always remember this as we continue to share the gospel. We pray as instructed for our President, our military, and the police to be safe and protected. We pray for the peace of Jerusalem, in the name of Jesus, amen.

Questions & Discussion

Do you know why Jesus is the only one? What can those other religion figures do for you? Discuss how to get to heaven.

DAY 63 – LET US OBEY

Scripture

Saying, Go unto this people, and say, Hearing ye shall hear, and shall not understand; and seeing ye shall see, and not perceive: For the heart of this people is waxed gross, and their ears are dull of hearing, and their eyes have they closed; lest they should see with their eyes, and hear with their ears, and understand with their heart, and should be converted, and I should heal them. Be it known therefore unto you, that the salvation of God is sent unto the Gentiles, and that they will hear it.

Acts 28:26-28 KJV

Gloria's Summary of Scripture

The Jewish people were known for being stubborn and hardheaded. They heard but couldn't comprehend. They saw but couldn't understand. God gave the Word to the Gentiles—non-Jewish people. Christians don't replace the Jewish people in God's eyes; we're added to the family.

LISTEN TO THEIR HEART
TALK ABOUT HOW IT BEATS
ALWAYS AND GOD HEARS EACH ONE

Prayer

Dear God, _____ wants to hear and understand Your Word and Your principles. We want our understanding enhanced so we don't miss Your blessings. We want the things of God You have for us and like the prophets of old, want to share with the people we meet. Help us learn from this scripture because we're willing. Thank You God for the scriptures. Thank You God for the promises You gave us. We are hearing, and we are learning. Help us apply this principle to all areas of our lives. Give us spiritual eyes, hearts and ears. We pray for the President, our military home and away, and the police officers, and all first responders for safety and protection. Lord, we pray for the Holy Land of Israel, for the peace of Jerusalem. In Jesus' name, amen.

Questions & Discussion

With open eyes and ears, and a willing heart are the keys to understanding the spiritual issues God has given us. Talk about a "willing heart" and what that means. It is giving all of their heart to God so He can do good works in them.

Day 64 – God Is Truth

Scripture

For the wrath of God is revealed from heaven against all ungodliness and unrighteousness of men, who hold the truth in unrighteousness; Because that which may be known of God is manifest in them; for God hath shewed it unto them.
Romans 1:18-19 KJV

Gloria's Summary of Scripture

God is angered by unholiness. People forget He is the God of perfection and it includes wrath. The unholy people will see His anger because they hear truth but ignore it. They make fun of the truth and live unholy lives. God's wrath follows.

TEACH YOUR CHILD TO BE BOLD
TALKING TO GOD
THEY CAN WHISPER TOO BECAUSE
HE HEARS THEM

Prayer

Dear Lord, help us live as You've taught us. Please help _____ be the person You want. Help us hear Your Word, read Your Word and live it too. Help us hear the value of the teaching at church. Help us use what we've learned so we can share the gospel with others. We want to know how to live and avoid Your wrath! We want to please You in everything we do. Our lives mean nothing without You in them, front and center. Thank You we are spared Your wrath because Your righteousness was given to us at the cross. We are covered by the blood of Jesus. He cleansed our hearts and prepared them to live as Christians. We pray for the peace of Jerusalem, and pray for the protection and safety of our President, our military, and the police. In Jesus' name we pray, amen.

Questions & Discussion

Teach them God is love, but in His perfection, He must be wrath too. Since He is perfect, His wrath is only one part of His personality. He is tenderness, mercy, goodness and many other good things. Ask them one thing they like best about Him.

DAY 65 – DIE ONE TIME

Scripture

And it is appointed unto men once to die, but after this the judgment: So Christ was once offered to bear the sins of many; and unto them that look for him shall he appear the second time without sin unto salvation.
Hebrews 9:27-28 KJV

Gloria's Summary of Scripture

Each person dies only one time, they then will face judgment of the good kind or the bad kind. If we are Christian, then we face a good judgment. Jesus died only once, and He is our pattern. When Jesus comes again, He is looking for those people who are eagerly awaiting His arrival as He greatly rewards them.

WITH A TENDER KISS ON THE CHIN
LET THEM KNOW
THIS IS THE FACE I LOVE

Prayer

Dear Jesus, thank You Jesus for the cross and the promises You made to _____. Thank You, You are still fulfilling those promises every day. Thank You and we praise You for being the God of our salvation. We're eagerly looking forward to the day You return to take us to heaven to be with You for eternity. We will understand the pattern You set for us in dying only one time. Other religions talk about living again differently, but it isn't truth and You only teach truth. Thank You Lord. We continue to pray for the peace of Jerusalem. We pray for the protection, safety, and wisdom for our President, our military home and away, and the police, and emergency responders to be safe from danger. We pray in Jesus' name, amen.

Questions & Discussion

Does judgment scare you? If so, why? Discuss and calm their possible fears. Because we are saved, we will be judged of the "good" kind and hear our names called from the Book of Life.

DAY 66 – HE IS WORTHY

Scripture

And I beheld, and I heard the voice of many angels round about the throne and the beasts and the elders: and the number of them was ten thousand times ten thousand, and thousands of thousands; Saying with a loud voice, Worthy is the Lamb that was slain to receive power, and riches, and wisdom, and strength, and honour, and glory, and blessing.

Revelation 5:11-12 KJV

Gloria's Summary of Scripture

John, the author of Revelation, sees thousands upon thousands of angels, biblical creatures and elders who are worshiping the Lamb, Jesus. They are all blessing Jesus and teaching us to follow their pattern.

COVER YOUR CHILD'S EYES
KISS THEM ON THE CHEEK
GO TO SLEEP MY PRECIOUS ONE
AND SLEEP WELL MY LITTLE LOVE

Prayer

Dear Jesus, yes, the Lamb is worthy! Help _____ remember each day how much You have done for us. Teach us to worship You as the beings in heaven worship you. Help us have hearts for You, to please You and give You great joy. Help us see the benefits of our worship. Help us teach others how to worship You and give You glory. It's all about You. Help us grow in the strength You give us to give You honor, power, riches, blessings, strength and wisdom. If we can learn these things, You will richly bless us. Thank You Jesus for Your sacrifice. We love you. We pray for the peace of Jerusalem, the safety and blessings of our military, the police, and for guidance, wisdom, and divine protection for the President. In Jesus' name we pray, amen.

Questions & Discussion

What do you think of angels? Having your own personal angel? Remember not to talk to them. We only talk to Jesus, God, and the Holy Spirit.

Day 67 – All Heaven Worships

Scripture

And every creature which is in heaven, and on the earth, and under the earth, and such as are in the sea, and all that are in them, heard I saying, Blessing, and honour, and glory, and power, be unto him that sitteth upon the throne, and unto the Lamb for ever and ever. And the four beasts said, Amen. And the four and twenty elders fell down and worshiped him that liveth for ever and ever.

Revelation 5:13-14 KJV

Gloria's Summary of Scripture

In the second part of this scripture in Revelation, we see John talking about all the animals worshiping Jesus telling us He has all these wonderful qualities. Twenty-four elders are in heaven and they fell to worship Jesus who lives forever.

KISS THE TOPS OF THEIR EARS
WHISPER
IN JESUS' NAME
I BLESS THIS CHILD TONIGHT

Prayer

Dear God, we worship You. _____ also gives You all blessings, honor, glory and power forever and ever. We join the animals in heaven as well as the elders who worship You. You are worthy of all adoration. You alone died on the cross for our sins. You alone are worthy to open the scrolls at the end of time. You alone are the One True Savior. We worship and praise You for all of it. Thank You for showing us there are animals in heaven. All the animals worship You. Everything in Your creation must love and worship You because You made us all. Thank you Lord! We continue to pray for the peace of Jerusalem, protection and wisdom for our President, for the police and our military both home and away. In Jesus' name, amen.

Questions & Discussion

This scripture gives us a look into eternity with knowledge we can hold onto while we are still here. Help them see this is a prayer too.

Day 68 – Speak Boldly

Scripture

For which I am an ambassador in bonds: that therein I may speak boldly, as I ought to speak.
Ephesians 6:20 KJV

Gloria's Summary of Scripture

Paul, the author of Ephesians was in chains for preaching, but he was well equipped to speak boldly regardless of the consequences. God expects us to speak boldly for Him, giving a response to those who are seeking the truth.

HOLD THEIR FEET
PRETEND TO "AIR WALK" THEM
LET THEM KNOW YOU BLESS
WHERE THESE FEET TAKE THEM

Prayer

Dear God, Lord help _____ to speak boldly. Thank You we have an example of how to do it. Paul preached in prison and out, every time he opened his mouth he was speaking about the glories of His Savior, Jesus. Teach us to speak boldly and without fear when we talk to others. Let us learn this lesson early so we don't stumble when we're given the chance to speak about You and Your goodness. Help us support other Christians who speak out about salvation and teaching the gospel. Teach us to be like You. We pray for the peace of Jerusalem, the protection and safety of our President, our military, and the police, including the fire department and emergency rescues. In Jesus' name, amen.

Questions & Discussion

Sometimes children speak boldly in their faith. It can be a fine line between being bold and being obnoxious, but confidence comes with practice. Teach them to know the difference.

DAY 69 – DECEPTION

Scripture

And Jesus answered and said unto them, Take heed that no man deceive you. For many shall come in my name, saying, I am Christ; and shall deceive many.
Matthew 24:4-5 KJV

Gloria's Summary of Scripture

Beware of hearing people say they are Jesus because He warned many will come in the last days saying they are, but they are lying. Many confused people populate the earth. You need to be aware of what God says in these scriptures.

KISS EACH ELBOW
ASK THEM IF THEY CAN KISS THEM
THEY CAN'T
GIGGLES AND HUGS

Prayer

Dear Jesus, You are the only God we need to hear and listen to. You don't lie; people do, _____ does not want to either. We want to know and tell the truth because You said the truth will set us free. We want that kind of freedom. We want to worship and give You the glory because there is no one like You. There was no one else at creation, only You Jesus, God the Father and the Holy Spirit. Help us understand the differences when we hear people say Jesus is here. When Jesus comes, we will know because we already love Him. We already have Jesus in our hearts. Help us be good Christians as we grow more and more in You. We pray for the peace of Jerusalem, for the safety and wisdom of our President, our military home and away, and the police and emergency responders. In Jesus' precious name, amen.

Questions & Discussion

Deceptions come whether we like it or not. In order to protect them from the lies the world tells, they need to better understand the Word of God. They will learn to know when they are being deceived by the people or the devil.

Day 70 – Jesus Is God

Scripture

He saith unto them, But whom say ye that I am? And Simon Peter answered and said, Thou art the Christ, the Son of the living God. And Jesus answered and said unto him, Blessed art thou, Simon Bar-Jona: for flesh and blood hath not revealed it unto thee, but my Father which is in heaven.
Matthew 16:15-17 KJV

Gloria's Summary of Scripture

Jesus spoke to Peter asking Who he thought Jesus was. He answered Jesus correctly because Jesus pointed out no one had told him, but the Father in heaven had revealed the truth to him. Jesus is God. In the next sentence, Jesus renamed Simon Peter to Peter.

LEARN GOODNIGHT
IN SIGN LANGUAGE TOGETHER
HAVE FUN WITH THIS NEW LANGUAGE
GIVE A KISS GOODNIGHT TOO

Prayer

Dear Jesus, You are God. You and the Father are One. Thank You for sending Your Holy Spirit to live inside us. The Holy Spirit is the part of You that lives inside us, helps us, guides us, and gives us knowledge and understanding. _____ also wants to know You fully and understand what You have to teach us. We know we're just learning, and we're willing to learn whatever You want to teach us. Help us be willing every day and help us remember these things. When we get confused, help us clearly remember what You've said. We want to please You and we will when we understand. We pray for the peace of Jerusalem, for the safety, divine protection, and blessings of our President, our military, and the police. In Jesus' mighty name, amen.

Questions & Discussion

Peter was such a "real" person, much like we are today. He stumbled, but he got many things right just as we do. Do they understand what the Son of the living God means? Explain how Jesus is God but the Triune of Jesus, God, the Holy Spirit are one.

DAY 71 — HE KNOWS ME

Scripture

O Lord, thou hast searched me, and known me. Thou knowest my downsitting and mine uprising; thou understandest my thought afar off. Thou compassest my path and my lying down, and art acquainted with all my ways. For there is not a word in my tongue, but, lo, O Lord, thou knowest it altogether.

Psalms 139:1-4 KJV

Gloria's Summary of Scripture

Psalm 139 is famous for being the story of how God knows us from the moment He first formed us in the womb. He knows us because He made us, unique in every way, though we share a common DNA with our parents.

LET THEM KNOW YOU ARE PROUD
OF THEIR ACCOMPLISHMENTS
AND YOU SEE THEIR DAILY EFFORTS
TO BE WHO GOD INTENDED

Prayer

Dear God, search _____ and know _____ as You did in the beginning when You formed us in mother's womb. Show us how big You are, Your majesty, Your beauty as we learn from the foundations of who we are, to grow to be more like You. You know our thoughts even before we speak. We know nothing yet, but we will as we get understanding and wisdom. We get closer to You every day if we just obey what You've taught us. Teach us to follow You because You have a plan for our lives and we just want to be obedient. We pray for the peace of Jerusalem, for the safety and protection of our President, our military both home and those on tours, and the police, and emergency responders. We pray in the precious name of Jesus, amen.

Questions & Discussion

God knows everything. Humans think they would like to be God, but not one could do it. As we serve God, our lives will be better, and longer. Talk about being formed in the womb and how life begins at conception as God knew us even before then.

DAY 72 – GOD IS EVERYWHERE

Scripture

Thou hast beset me behind and before, and laid thine hand upon me. Such knowledge is too wonderful for me; it is high, I cannot attain unto it. Whither shall I go from thy Spirit? Or whither shall I flee from thy presence? If I ascend up into heaven, thou art there: if I make my bed in hell, behold, thou art there.
Psalms 139:5-8 KJV

Gloria's Summary of Scripture

God has gone before us and behind us with His hand upon us. It is overwhelming to consider. If our Spirit goes to heaven, He is there. The writer, David says God is present in hell. God is not in hell, but His Spirit comes and goes as He pleases.

PICK UP THEIR KNEES
BEND THEM TO YOUR LIPS
LET THEM KNOW YOU AND JESUS
BLESS THEIR PRAYING KNEES

Prayer

Dear God, Lord please help _____ understand how You can be everywhere at once. We have been taught You are three in one; Jesus and the Holy Spirit are God with You, so it gets confusing. The word is "omnipresent" and means everywhere at one time, it is more than our minds can really understand, but with Your help, we can. This means if You are everywhere, we will never be out of Your reach, or out of the reach of the Holy Spirit. That's good news! We believe You can do anything, thank You for always being there for us. We pray for the President, our military, and the police to be out of danger. We pray for the peace of Jerusalem. In Jesus' name, amen.

Questions & Discussion

If there are questions you don't have answers for, ask God together and since they have been learning to listen for the small still voice of the Lord, they should listen with faith for an answer. He is anywhere, everywhere, available all the time.

DAY 73 – PROTECTION

Scripture

If I take the wings of the morning, and dwell in the uttermost parts of the sea; Even there shall thy hand lead me, and thy right hand shall hold me. If I say, Surely the darkness shall cover me; even the night shall be light about me. Yea, the darkness hideth not from thee; but the night shineth as the day: the darkness and the light are both alike to thee.
Psalms 139:9-12 KJV

Gloria's Summary of Scripture

There is no darkness in God. Everywhere He is there is light. The Psalmist understood this and says even in darkness God is with him and the night becomes like day because God is his protector.

> REMIND THEM TO LOVE OTHERS
> AS CHRIST LOVES THEM
> TREAT OTHERS
> AS YOU WISH TO BE TREATED

Prayer

Dear Father God, we want faith like David had! We want to be like him when he understood so many things about You. It's because he drew close to You that You drew closer to him. As _____ draws closer and closer to You, it will happen for _____ too. Thank You God You have these great big plans for us, like You did for David, a man after Your own heart. Make us like David. Make us like Jesus. As we grow, show us the plans You have for us since You know us so well. Thank You God. We pray for the peace of Jerusalem, for the protection, safety and special blessings of our President, our military, and police officers, including all emergency responders. In the name of Jesus, amen.

Questions & Discussion

Faith grows as it is watered by the Word of God. When they hear truths, pray truths, and read it for themselves, it becomes their own faith. Practice makes it stronger. Talk about heaven being light all the time, no darkness, God is light.

Day 74 – Wonderfully Made

Scripture

For thou hast possessed my reins: thou hast covered me in my mother's womb, I will praise thee; for I am fearfully and wonderfully made: marvelous are thy works; and that my soul knoweth right well. My substance was not hid from thee, when I was made in secret, and curiously wrought in the lowest parts of the earth.

Psalms 139:13-15 KJV

Gloria's Summary of Scripture

Here is the essence of the Psalm; meditate on this one and when you realize not only did God know you before you were formed in secret, but He knew all about you and who you would become. Praise God! Remember Adam was formed from the dust of the earth.

As you tuck them in tightly
Whisper softly in their ear
I think you are pretty special

Prayer

Dear God, we give You thanks, first of all, because You are such a good God. You've been with us all the time, even while we were in mommy's tummy. While we were growing inside her, You knew who _____ already was, and You have called us to be Your children too. Thank You for letting us grow to this size and watching us while we learn more about You. Help us get this information at church and help us share it with others. Help us tell it truthfully, as we want to tell the story without making mistakes. You're so awesome because You knew us before we were ever made. We pray for the safety of the President, our military, the police, and we pray for the peace of Jerusalem as You've asked us to. All in the name of Jesus, amen.

Questions & Discussion

God loves children, He loves yours, He loves you. His love will grow your children and teach them valuable lessons for life because they are fearfully and wonderfully made.

DAY 75 – A GREAT CREATION

Scripture

Thine eyes did see my substance, yet being unperfect; and in thy book all my members were written, which in continuance were fashioned, when as yet there was none of them. How precious also are thy thoughts unto me, O God! How great is the sum of them! If I should count them, they are more in number than the sand: when I awake, I am still with thee.

Psalms 139:16-18 KJV

Gloria's Summary of Scripture

God saw you before you were born, and He recorded who you are. Each day was planned out for you before you were ever born. Life is incredibly precious and He thinks about you all the time.

LET THEM KNOW YOU APPRECIATE
WHEN THEY REMEMBER TO OBEY
THEY WILL GROW UP AND KNOW HOW
MUCH THEY LEARNED FROM IT

Prayer

Dear God, You are great and greatly to be praised. _____ wants You to know how much we love You and how much we thank You for the love You have for us even before we were born. Our lives were important to You even when we were in our mother's tummy. We were living beings even then. Thank You that our mom loves us. Thank You God we are learning how important life is to You. With praises, glory, honor and blessings to You for the great God You are. We continue to pray for the President, our military home and away, the police to be protected, and for the peace of Jerusalem. In Jesus' name, amen.

Questions & Discussion

God knitted us together and we were a substance He calls life. When you can age appropriately show photos of a growing child in the womb, talk them through the stages. Its amazing to learn. Life is precious to God. All innocent life is to be protected.

DAY 76 – ENEMIES OF GOD

Scripture

Surely thou wilt slay the wicked, O God: depart from me therefore, ye bloody men. For they speak against thee wickedly, and thine enemies take thy name in vain. Do not I hate them, O Lord, that hate thee? And am not I grieved with those that rise up against thee?
Psalms 139:19-21 KJV

Gloria's Summary of Scripture

Today, hatred is everywhere, but this discussion between David and God is important. We see here David was concerned about the kind of hatred he saw toward God's magnificence and tenderness toward all life.

> SLEEP COZY AND
> HAVE SWEET DREAMS
> GIVE THEM A BIG HUG AND KISS
> GOODNIGHT AT LIGHTS OUT

Prayer

Dear God, Lord help _____ understand all innocent life is precious. Let us comprehend the love You feel toward babies, You love us, You love all children and families. You said life is precious. You said we should not murder. You said it's evil and we are allowed to hate those sins. We believe what You said in Your Word. Help us share this truth with other people. Help us share the gospel and include the fact, life is valuable when we do. Thank You God. We continue to pray for the peace of Jerusalem, for the protection and safety of our President, our military, and the police and emergency responders. We pray in Jesus' holy name, amen.

Questions & Discussion

We are fighting against all the principalities and powers in heavenly places. The devil is seeking to destroy while he is here on earth. Remind them how the devil is out to win their souls and the only way to not be tempted is to stay daily rooted in the Word of God.

Day 77 – Know My Heart

Scripture

I hate them with perfect hatred: I count them mine enemies. Search me, O God, and know my heart: try me, and know my thoughts: And see if there be any wicked way in me, and lead me in the way everlasting.

Psalms 139:22-24 KJV

Gloria's Summary of Scripture

In the final sequence of this Psalm, David remembers the perfect hatred he has for God's enemies. He asks God to search his heart to see if there is any wickedness in him and show him the way to eternity. In other words, point out my faults, God.

LET THEM KNOW
HOW PRECIOUS THEY ARE
MADE BY GOD IN ALL HIS GLORY
HE DOESN'T MAKE MISTAKES

Prayer

Dear God, we come together asking You to show us Your enemies. We have learned hatred for sin is the only hate allowed, we are not to hate people. King David asked for You to search his heart and _____ wants You to do that for _____ too. We want to be pure in all our ways. We want to please You and enjoy the life You set for us. Search us and see if there are any displeasing thoughts and point them out to us. Lead us on the path of righteousness and holiness Jesus taught us to want. Tonight, again we pray for the peace of Jerusalem, the safety and protection for the President, our military both home and overseas, and the police. In Jesus' holy name, amen.

Questions & Discussion

Hate the sin, not the person. Teach the children the difference because we all sin, it just may be a different sin. We who have learned better are held to a higher standard. Jesus is pleased with them for learning this. Discuss this.

DAY 78 – BE THANKFUL

Scripture

O give thanks unto the Lord; for he is good: for his mercy endureth for ever.
Psalms 136:1 KJV

Gloria's Summary of Scripture

Psalm 136 contains phrases; each one is finished with praising God for his endurance, or in other versions, His faithfulness enduring forever. That's just how good He is!

AS YOU TURN OFF THE LIGHT
AND CLOSE THE DOOR
CALL OUT TO THEM BY NAME
I BLESS YOU IN THE NAME OF JESUS

Prayer

Dear God, let _____ remember how faithful You are in all things. You give us the things we need throughout the day. We are blessed with a place to be safe, friends, loving parents, food, the bible and each day we're thankful for all of them. Sometimes we don't remember to thank You, but we have so many things to be thankful for. But most of all, we're thankful You are faithful, and You endure forever. We don't have to worry about life because You are always here with us. You won't ever fail us. All we have to do is ask and Your help is there. We pray for the peace of Jerusalem, for the safety of the President, our military's men and women, the police officers, and emergency responders. We pray in the mighty name of Jesus, amen.

Questions & Discussion

Teaching children to be thankful and recognize their gifts from God is a crucial part of growing up to be great adults. Enjoy giving and be grateful for what we have is pure joy.

Day 79 – Don't Fear

Scripture

Fear thou not; for I am with thee: be not dismayed; for I am thy God: I will strengthen thee; yea, I will help thee; yea, I will uphold thee with the right hand of my righteousness.
Isaiah 41:10 KJV

Gloria's Summary of Scripture

365 times the bible says, "fear not" and that's enough for each day of the year. God says not to fear because He is our God and He will strengthen us and hold us up because He is good.

> HOLD THEIR HANDS
> KISS EACH OF THEIR PINKIES
> GOD IS SO AWESOME HE CARES EVEN
> IF YOU HAVE A SCRATCH

Prayer

Dear God, if we fear anything, is it wrong? Yes, You say not to fear. _____ has nothing to fear because You are here with us, day and night. We thank You for Your promise, though we won't always be strong, we will try. We will walk in the promise of no fear every day. You are always with us because You're a good God Who is faithful and just and always ready beside us. Our only fear is if we've done something to displease You and have not repented of our sin. We now know the right thing to do, so help us do it every time. Thank You God. We continue to pray for the peace of Jerusalem, for the protection and safety of the President, our military, and police. In Jesus' name, amen.

Questions & Discussion

F.E.A.R. or False Evidence Appearing Real is fear that can overcome us if we are not aware of it. Learn to rebuke fear. "In Jesus' name, I rebuke fear," anytime you feel it on you. Ask God to surround you in protection and Jesus to be by your side.

DAY 80 – TRUST IN HIM

Scripture

He that dwelleth in the secret place of the Most High shall abide under the shadow of the Almighty. I will say of the Lord, He is my refuge and my fortress: my God; in him will I trust.
Psalms 91:1-2 KJV

Gloria's Summary of Scripture

This is an old song, but a great song. Trusting God is of great importance in life. There are times when you'll need His shelter and protection, and He will be there.

I LOVE YOU SOOOO MUCH...HOW MUCH
HUG THEM BIG
WITH WIDE OUTSTRETCHED ARMS
THIIIIIIS MUCH

Prayer

Dear God, Lord please help _____ call on You when trouble comes. You are a place of security and health and a high tower where we are always safe. Help us share the good news by sharing the gospel and tell others how big You are. You are a wonderful God and we know it. Encourage us to share truth with other people who don't know You because we trust You. Every day we get a chance to tell You just how much we trust You and love You. Thank You for always taking us in when we need it. Lord we pray the Holy Land of Israel, for the peace of Jerusalem. We pray for the protection of our President, our military home and away, and the police, and first responders. We pray in the name above every name, Jesus, amen.

Questions & Discussion

God doesn't have wings, but interestingly, in the days when the Ark of the Covenant was with them, they would put it in the sun and when the shadow rested on the ground, they would be in that shadow to ask for God's special protection. Neat thought, discuss this.

Day 81 – Truth Is A Shield

Scripture

Surely he shall deliver thee from the snare of the fowler, and from the noisome pestilence. He shall cover thee with his feathers, and under his wings shall thou trust: his truth shall be thy shield and buckler. Thou shalt not be afraid for the terror by night; nor for the arrow that flieth by day; Nor for the pestilence that walketh in darkness; nor for the destruction that wasteth at noonday.
Psalms 91:3-6 KJV

Gloria's Summary of Scripture

God is always there to protect us. There is no pestilence that can harm us in darkness or midday because we trust the God of faithfulness. No, God doesn't have feathers—but a soft protection as we snuggle close "under" the wings, being the safest spot near God's underbelly (a baby chick with her mother).

HAVE YOUR CHILD PICK A FAVORITE
SONG FOR YOU TO SING
ENJOY THIS TIME TOGETHER
CONTINUE TO HUM IT AS YOU LEAVE

Prayer

Dear God our Father in heaven, _____ has Your promises and Your faithfulness, and truth that does not ever fail us—ever. We rely on Your Word to tell us the truth, who You are, and what You do for us all the time. If only we could always remember! Help us learn these things so we're able to know them when we need them. You alone are the One Who can get us through. Thank You for our parents and teachers who help guide us. Thank You for our blessings, comfort, protection and our defense. We pray for the protection of our President, our military both home and on special duty overseas, the police officers, and emergency responders. We ask for the peace of Jerusalem. In Jesus' name, amen.

Questions & Discussion

When mothers become "momma bears," that is the same way God feels about His children. He wants us to know His truth for protection so we don't get caught in bad situations.

DAY 82 – EVIL GETS PUNISHED

Scripture

A thousand shall fall at thy side, and ten thousand at thy right hand; but it shall not come nigh thee. Only with thine eyes shalt thou behold and see the reward of the wicked. Because thou hast made the Lord, which is my refuge, even the Most High, thy habitation; There shall no evil befall thee, neither shall any plague come nigh thy dwelling.

Psalms 91:7-10 KJV

Gloria's Summary of Scripture

Though thousands of people might fall at your side with people dying everywhere around you, you will be rescued. Your eyes will see how the wicked are punished. Once the Lord is your safety, no evil will come near you or your home.

WITH A BIG HUG
REASSURE THEM YOU PROTECT THEM
GOD PROTECTS THEM
AND THEY DON'T HAVE TO WORRY

Prayer

Dear God, protect us dear Lord. In all we do, give _____ Your protection You promised over and over. Thank You, You are faithful even when we aren't. Thank You for forgiveness and blessings, for comfort, tenderness and mercy, and for Your grace that covers multitudes of sins we didn't mean to do. Let no evil come near us as we follow You closely. Thank You for punishing the evil people and blessing those who follow You. Thank You for our salvation through Jesus. We pray for the peace of Jerusalem, for the divine protection of our President, our military, and police, first responders. We pray In Jesus' name, amen.

Questions & Discussion

Does this mean we are protected? Yes, this Psalm is one of protection. We use this prayer format and it helps when people are sick. Nothing can get to us. Trust Him in your prayers.

Day 83 – Fierce Protection

Scripture

For he shall give his angels charge over thee, to keep thee in all thy ways. They shall bear thee up in their hands, lest thou dash thy foot against a stone. Thou shalt tread upon the lion and adder: the young lion and the dragon shalt thou trample under feet.
Psalms 91:11-13 KJV

Gloria's Summary of Scripture

There is no protector like God! He's sending angels to cover you, to keep watch. You can safely walk among dangerous creatures you can't see, and you will have the power to keep them away.

> WHISPER AND SEE IF THEY GUESS
> TE QUIERO IN SPANISH
> ICH LIEBE DICH IN GERMAN
> JE T'AIME IN FRENCH
> I LOVE YOU IN ENGLISH

Prayer

Dear Jesus, thank You for sending angels to surround _____. We thank You they are all around us and each person has their own. We're special and they know it. They keep watch over us so we don't fall into danger, but to help us recognize it when we see it, and thank You we can walk safely with You on our daily journey. Thank You for the protection You have over us and for that of the angels. We can call upon You at any time and we know You'll be there. Tonight, we continue to pray for the peace of Jerusalem, for the protection and wisdom of our President, our military men and women, police, and emergency responders. In the mighty name of Jesus, amen.

Questions & Discussion

Remind them not to talk to angels, but trust they are always there to protect them. Some people say they have seen angels. They may step in and show themselves if it is necessary. God does all kinds of things to get our attention. We must look and listen.

DAY 84 – GOOD NEWS

Scripture

Because he hath set his love upon me, therefore will I deliver him: I will set him on high, because he hath known my name. He shall call upon me, and I will answer him: I will be with him in trouble; I will deliver him, and honour him. With long life will I satisfy him, and shew him my salvation.
Psalms 91:14-16 KJV

Gloria's Summary of Scripture

What better deal can we get than this? Because we love him, He will deliver us, be with us in trouble, give us honor (rewards) and He will give us a long, satisfying life and show us salvation!

KISS YOUR LIPS WITH YOUR INDEX
FINGER AND TOUCH THEIR LIPS
AS YOU DO LET THEM KNOW
YOU LOVE THE SOUNDS THEY MAKE

Prayer

Dear God, hear the prayer _____ has just for You tonight. We thank You, there is nothing in the universe like You. You are the Only God! We have so much to be thankful for. You not only forgive us of our sins, but we are honored because we love You. You give us a long life because we're saved. If we are in any trouble, we just need to call on You and there You will be. You don't ever leave us but You love us to ask, and You jump to our needs. There's nothing more precious than You, God. Help us remember this all the days of our lives, and to share with our friends, teachers, everyone we meet. Let us be bold! Tonight Lord, we continue to pray for the peace of Jerusalem, for the protection of our President, our military, and the police. Thank You God. In Jesus' name we pray, amen.

Questions & Discussion

When kids fully understand this and use it, there is nothing stopping them. It is the high prize Paul talked about. Being close to God is the best thing we can ever do. Discuss this with them before you tuck them in.

DAY 85 – LAMB'S BOOK OF LIFE

Scripture

And they sung a new song, saying, Thou art worthy to take the book, and to open the seals thereof: for thou wast slain, and hast redeemed us to God by thy blood out of every kindred, and tongue, and people, and nation; And hast made us unto our God kings and priests: and we shall reign on the earth.
Revelation 5:9-10 KJV

Gloria's Summary of Scripture

The Lamb's Book Of Life can only be opened by Jesus. None other is worthy. The elders fell before Jesus with the beautiful prayers of the saints in their hands—these, are the ones you are praying now. Jesus gives us the ability to rule and reign with Him because He loves us.

TICKLE THEM GENTLY
LET THEM KNOW
THEY ARE LOVED
MORE THAN THEY WILL EVER KNOW

Prayer

Dear Jesus, worthy are You Lord. Only You can open the book. All the people in the whole universe who have died and gone to heaven, out of all the people ever in time, You are the One Who can. Thank You _____ understands how incredible You are. Thank You we're Your children, who love You and want to please You. There is such a feeling of warmth and love pouring out over us and we can't thank You enough. Your salvation is a wonderful thing, it's all about You Jesus. We pray for the peace of Jerusalem, for blessings and the safe security of our President, for our military home and away, and the police, and first responders to always be safe. In Jesus' name, amen.

Questions & Discussion

This is an amazing vision John had. We are blessed to be able to see what God showed John all those years ago. We can share this with our children. God will not forget who you are or what you are doing. He will bless you for it.

DAY 86 – STAY FREE

Scripture

Stand fast therefore in the liberty wherewith Christ hath made us free, and be not entangled again with the yoke of bondage.
Galatians 5:1 KJV

Gloria's Summary of Scripture

God expects us to stay free. He's given us freedom but it's up to us not to take back the chains of enslavement or bondage we came out of. Reverting to the old us isn't wise. We must continue to grow, not remain still in our spirit.

KISS THE LITTLE ONE ON THE NOSE
SNIFF IN AND OUT IN AND OUT
TELL THEM THAT THEIR NOSE
IS JUST SO CUTE

Prayer

Dear God, show _____ how to enjoy the freedoms You gave us in Your Word. Help us stay out of trouble that might take us back where we first started. We don't want to have to start all over asking for forgiveness for sins when we don't always walk with You. When we walk with You, just as You've desired for us, we don't get into trouble. We will stay free and live the best lives You had in mind when You made us in our mommy's womb. Thank You God for all the reminders You will give us. We pray for the peace of Jerusalem, for the protection of our President, our military and police. In Jesus' name we pray, amen.

Questions & Discussion

Nothing is ever really free. Freedom is not free. Jesus paid the price for our freedom on the cross with His death. Our military fight for the freedoms we Americans have. Our ancestors fought for our lands and our rights by the Constitution. So stay free.

DAY 87 – FORGIVENESS REMINDER

Scripture

For if ye forgive men their trespasses, your heavenly Father will also forgive you: But if ye forgive not men their trespasses, neither will your Father forgive your trespasses.
Matthew 6:14-15 KJV

Gloria's Summary of Scripture

Remember to forgive others and it is also important to forgive yourselves after you repent of sins. God has wiped the slate clean and you are not to hold onto these old things, it helps you live in your freedom.

ASK IF THEY HAVE HEARD FROM
JESUS OR THE HOLY SPIRIT
IF NOT
LISTEN QUIETLY NOW TOGETHER

Prayer

Dear God, thank You for reminding _____ to forgive others. When we forgive them, You will also forgive us. We need forgiveness all the time, and so do other people. Help us walk in forgiveness all the time. When our feelings get hurt, help us remember other people are sinners and need forgiveness too. Help us share with others why we forgive easily, because of You. Teach us the value of forgiveness so when we grow up, we better understand how to forgive quickly even when it is tough to do. Thank You Jesus for Your sacrifice. We continue to faithfully pray for the peace of Jerusalem, for the continued protection of our President, our military, police, and all first responders. In Jesus' precious name, amen.

Questions & Discussion

Prayer and forgiveness are really important elements in our walk with Jesus. If we can remember these things, our lives can be much easier with a few daily prayers to set us free.

DAY 88 – JOY IS STRENGTH

Scripture

…for this day is holy unto our Lord: neither be ye sorry; for the joy of the Lord is your strength.
Nehemiah 8:10b KJV

Gloria's Summary of Scripture

There is a difference between joy and happiness. Your joy rests on God's joy and it comes from within, and is a constant gladness with cause to rejoice, only found in God's restoration of us. Happiness is only temporary, but joy is eternal.

> HUG AND TELL THEM YOU SAW
> SOMETHING THEY DID TODAY
> AND YOU ARE SO PROUD OF THEM
> EXPLAIN WHAT YOU SAW

Prayer

Dear God, give _____ joy resting upon Your joy. Help us go through life with an attitude of joy and an attitude of thankfulness because of Who You are and Your work in restoring us. It's not what we have done that is so great, but what You have done since the beginning of time. Thank You for making us in Your image. Thank You for calling us one of Your children. Help us remember joy in You is a strength. When we are not having a good day, we can turn it around if we think about how You give us joy within and it makes us strong. We pray for the peace of Jerusalem, for wisdom and safe protection of our President, our military, and police. In Jesus' mighty name we pray, amen.

Questions & Discussion

"I give my hands to do your work, the joy of the Lord is my strength," some lyrics from an old song. These help us remember scripture lines when we can sing them.

DAY 89 – OBEY

Scripture

Behold, to obey is better than sacrifice, and to hearken than the fat of rams.

1 Samuel 15:22b KJV

Gloria's Summary of Scripture

In this scripture, Samuel discussed what was important. He declared obedience was better than a sacrifice of animals. God prefers we are obedient. Anyone can make a sacrifice. We look at it like this though, obedience IS our sacrifice.

> EXPLAIN HOW DEEP
> THE OCEAN REALLY IS
> TELL THEM YOU
> LOVE THEM THAT DEEPLY

Prayer

Dear God, teach _____ to hear You immediately. Speak to us often so we know Your voice, only then we can obey. You've called us to listen and we want to, and as we learn to recognize Your voice, we will be able to hear when You speak. Whether it's in our minds or out loud, we want to hear You, we don't want to miss any instruction. We can sometimes make mistakes when we first learn how to hear You, because we may mistake it for our own thoughts, but as we practice, we will get better. God, hear our prayers and help us. As we do, we continue to pray for the peace of Jerusalem, for the protection of the President, our military, police, and emergency responders. We pray in Jesus' holy name, amen.

Questions & Discussion

Ever feel a funny feeling in your tummy? Maybe you call it a "gut" feeling? It is the Holy Spirit speaking to you, guiding you through your feelings and thoughts. It is important to look, listen, and pray about things if you are not sure. We want to obey at all times.

DAY 90 – STRONG WARNING

Scripture

For rebellion is as the sin of witchcraft, and stubbornness is as iniquity and idolatry.

1 Samuel 15:23a KJV

Gloria's Summary of Scripture

Rebellion is like witchcraft which is evil, and stubbornness is a purposeful sin, and is like worshiping idols. These warnings are straight to the point. Be very wary about seeing a rebellious streak in your children and hastily pray against it.

> SPEAK SWEET NOTHINGS TO YOUR CHILD DAILY
> TO SHOW A DEEP LOVE
> THOSE NOTHINGS ARE REALLY SOMETHINGS
> VERY SPECIAL THEY WILL REMEMBER FOREVER

Prayer

Dear God, these are very important warnings, so we need Your constant help to avoid the sin of rebellion and stubbornness. When parents tell us to do something we don't want to do, help _____ be obedient and not fall into sin. We know of games and TV shows or movies with witchcraft, and we want to avoid those, as You have warned us against this. We praise You God because we can't do anything that will keep us from You, so we need protection. We have been obedient to pray for the peace of Jerusalem and praying for our President to have wisdom and be safe. We've prayed for our military men and women, the police officers to be safe and out of danger, and for all first responders to be protected as well. We ask you to honor these things. We pray in Jesus' holy name, amen.

Questions & Discussion

Rebellion is a serious sin. Stubbornness has big consequences. Keep praying and reading the Word of God to continue to grow and please God, you have His attention! Congratulations its been 90 days of praying with the children.

Thank You

Train Up a Child in the Way He Should Go... Proverbs 22:6
90 Day Bible Study / Prayer Guide

We thank you for taking part in this book with your children. It might be fun for you to repeat the next 90 days if they really enjoyed learning. Remember they do well with repetition. If you take notes on the back page you will love seeing the growth over the next 90 days.

We are so glad you chose to spend valuable time teaching your children the Word of God and praying with them. Our hope is you have enjoyed sharing scriptures and prayers with them and they have asked questions to help nudge your desire for further reading the Word.

Many blessings to you and your family. We pray for you in the name of Jesus to ask God's abundant blessings fall on all of you.

If this prayer guide has impacted you and your family, we would love to hear about it!
You can leave a review and comment for others to also be inspired. Share this book with your church family and Sunday school teachers. You may find it helpful to talk with a pastor about it. If you are interested in more books by Gloria Huntington, please search Amazon by author for other titles.

If you would like prayer, or have questions, please email prayerwithgloriahuntington@gmail.com

About The Author

Gloria Huntington is a grandmother whose grandchildren lived too far away to tuck into bed every night.

She loves the Word of God and would have loved to share with her grandchildren had it worked out just right, however she did teach her daughter Nicole how to share with her children so the boys grew up with nightly prayers and the Word of God.

She would like to encourage parents to make a routine kids will look forward to each night and this will train them up in the way they should go to follow God all of their lives.

She loves her local church, her pastor and the prayer team she prays with. She meets with the prayer team once a week for an afternoon session.

Gloria has been a born-again Christian since 1982. She has been blessed with a full life, complete with most importantly her time with God, a loving family, and her precious animals; all types of animals are drawn to her.

Her other interests have included some volunteering in her community, politics, hosting a radio show and writing books.

She wants to thank her husband Johnny E. for his love and support, her daughter Nicole and husband Jim for their work in production.

NOTES

Made in United States
Orlando, FL
07 August 2023

35832613R00057